W9-CDU-657

THE SOVIET UNION

THE SOVIET UNION

AN INTRODUCTION

GEORGE ALEXANDER LENSEN

NEW YORK

APPLETON-CENTURY-CROFTS
DIVISION OF MEREDITH PUBLISHING COMPANY

667-1
Library of Congress Card Number: 67-25435
PRINTED IN THE UNITED STATES OF AMERICA
E 55320

ACKNOWLEDGMENTS

(*Page numbers given are those of this volume.*)

p. 125 From ON SOCIALIST REALISM, by Abram Tertz. © Copyright 1960 by Pantheon Books. Reprinted by permission of Random House, Inc.

pp. 125-126 "Mowers in the Line of Fire" by Valerij Bryusov, from *Russian Poetry 1917-1955*, trans. by Jack Lindsay (London: The Bodley Head Ltd., 1957), pp. 23-24. Reprinted by permission.

p. 126 From ON SOCIALIST REALISM, by Abram Tertz. © Copyright 1960 by Pantheon Books. Reprinted by permission of Random House, Inc.

p. 130 Copyright 1950 by Babette Deutsch. Reprinted from PUSHKIN: HIS LIFE AND TIMES, by Henri Troyat, by permission of Pantheon Books, a Division of Random House, Inc.

pp. 130, 132 From Vera Aleksandrova, *A History of Soviet Literature 1917-1962* (Garden City, N.Y.: Doubleday & Company, Inc., 1963), p. 332. Reprinted by permission of the publisher and G. Bell & Sons, Ltd., London.

pp. 132-133 "The Nobel Prize" by Boris Pasternak, from *Poems* by Boris Pasternak, trans. by Eugene M. Kayden (Yellow Springs, Ohio: The Antioch Press, 1964), p. 300. Copyright 1964 by Eugene M. Kayden. Reprinted by permission.

pp. 134-135 "Simplicity" by Semyon Kirsonov, from *Russian Poetry 1917-1955*, trans. by Jack Lindsay (London: The Bodley Head Ltd., 1957), pp. 136-137. Reprinted by permission.

TO MY FATHER

PREFACE

Many Americans think of the Soviet Union and of communism only in terms of subversion and treason, slave labor camps, and military aggression. Others, in an attempt to be fair, see the Soviet Union only as the champion of the working class and as the pioneer in space exploration. The difficulty of appraising the Soviet Union justly is due not only to the emotion generated by these opposite views and to our national involvement in the defense of Berlin, Korea, Vietnam, and other places but results also from the lack of reliable data.

It is no easy matter to go to the Soviet Union and "see for yourself." Although tourism is encouraged, only certain cities are open to foreigners. The country at large remains closed. If you work for the United States embassy or an American newspaper you may receive permission to travel more widely, but relatively few Russians will risk associating with you. Visiting artists, professors, and graduate students are in the best position to mingle with Russians and soak up the atmosphere, but only a limited number in this category are exchanged each year.

Whether you go as a tourist or a long-term visitor, you will be impressed by the beauty of Leningrad, the architecture of the Moscow Kremlin, the artistic perfection of the Russian ballet, and the magnificent staging of the opera. If you are a tourist with no background in Russian history, you will probably marvel at these "Soviet" accomplishments. If you are a student of history, on the other hand, you will be aware that these are Russian achievements. The Soviet Union was built on the remains of the Russian Empire; it has inherited many of its traditions and problems. It has "Communized" some, and been "Russianized" by others.

This book describes the Soviet Union and the Communist system without losing sight of the Russian people. It pays particular attention to Russian culture, the dominant influence in Soviet society. As President John F. Kennedy stated:

> No government or social system is so evil that its people must be considered as lacking in virtue. As Americans, we find Communism profoundly repugnant as a negation of personal freedom and dignity. But we can still hail the Russian people for their many achievements—in science and space, in economic and industrial growth, in culture [and] in acts of courage.

The photographs in this book were taken by me in April and May of 1965. I am indebted to the Inter-University Committee on Travel Grants for making possible a more extended stay in the Soviet Union in one of the dormitories of Leningrad State University in 1961. I wish to thank Professor W. A. Douglas Jackson of the University of Washington in Seattle, Professor Loren Graham of Columbia University, and Professor Essie Jacobs of the University of Miami for reading the entire manuscript and making many valuable suggestions. I am particularly grateful to Professor Alexander Dallin of Columbia University, whose friendly criticism did much to temper my approach. Miss Kim Maddox, a young old friend, helped keep the text lucid. Miss Evon Streetman of the Florida State University and Mr. Lee Ray Dunn of Parks-Streetman Photography designed my darkroom and advised me generously on getting the most out of my negatives. Needless to say, I alone am responsible for the views and interpretations expressed in these pages.

G.A.L.

CONTENTS

BARENTS SEA
Novaya Zemlya
KARA SEA
WHITE SEA
Arkhangelsk
Ladoga
L. Onega
BALTIC SEA
Tallin
ESTONIAN S.S.R.
Leningrad
LATVIAN
Riga
Dvina
LITHUANIAN S.S.R.
Vilniuso
Northern Dvina
Minsk
BYELORUSSIAN S.S.R.
Pripyat
Moskva
Moscow
RUSSIAN
URALS
Ob
Irtysh
Kazan
Kiev
UKRAINIAN S.S.R.
MOLDAVIAN S.S.R.
Kishinev
Kharkov
Donets
Dnieper
Kuibyshev
Cheliabinsk
Novosibirsk
Omsk
Volga
Don
Rostov
Volgograd (Stalingrad)
Ural
Simforopol
Novorossiisk
KAZAKH S.S.R.
CAUCASUS
GEORGIAN S.S.R.
Tbilisi
CASPIAN SEA
Aral Sea
Syr-Darya
L. Balkash
Yerevan
ARMENIAN S.S.R.
AZERBAIDZHAN S.S.R.
Baku
Amu-Darya
Chu
Ili
Alma Ata
Frunze
L. Issy-Kul
KIRGHIZ S.S.R.
Tashkent
TURKMEN S.S.R.
UZBEK S.S.R.
TIEN SHAN
Ashkhabad
TADZHIK S.S.R.
Dushambe
PAMIRS

THE SOVIET UNION

GEOGRAPHICAL FEATURES AND POLITICAL SUBDIVISIONS

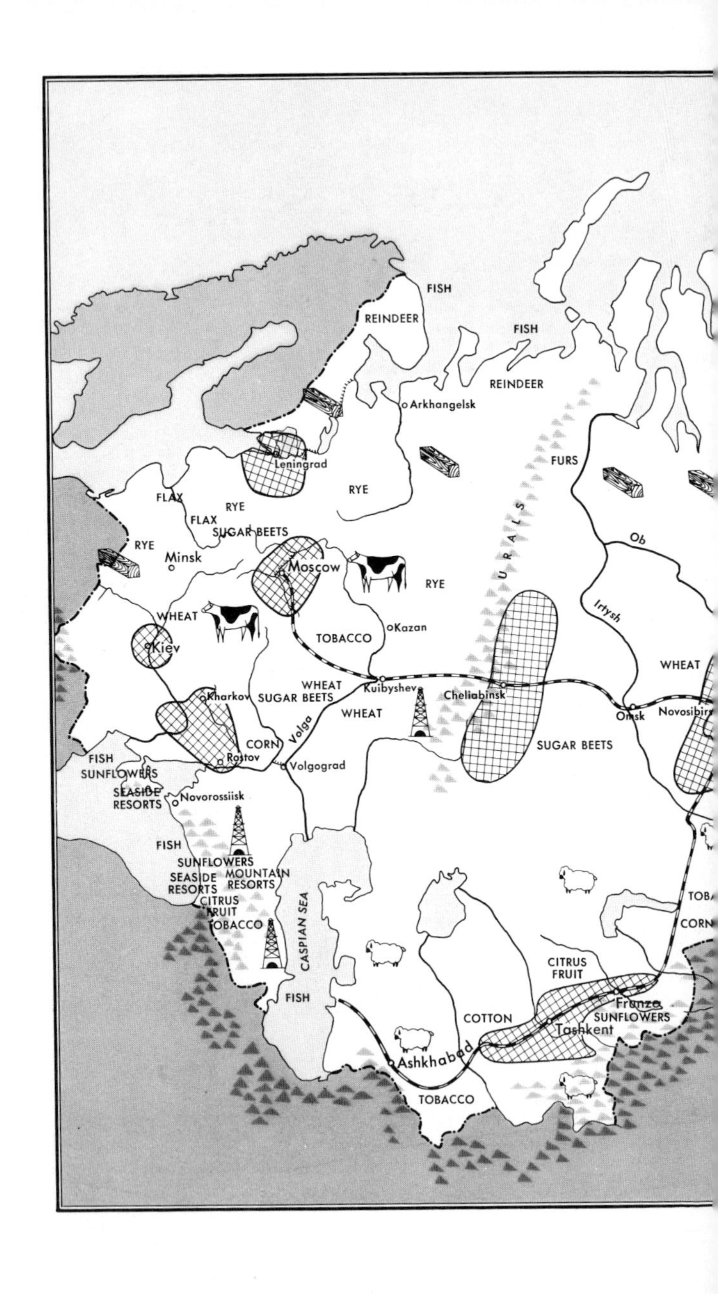
FISH
REINDEER
FISH
REINDEER
Arkhangelsk
Leningrad
RYE
FURS
FLAX
RYE
FLAX
SUGAR BEETS
URALS
Ob
RYE
Minsk
Moscow
RYE
Irtysh
WHEAT
Kiev
TOBACCO
Kazan
WHEAT
Kharkov
SUGAR BEETS
WHEAT
Kuibyshev
Cheliabinsk
Omsk
Novosibir
WHEAT
Volga
CORN
Rostov
SUGAR BEETS
FISH
SUNFLOWERS
Volgograd
SEASIDE RESORTS
Novorossiisk
FISH
SUNFLOWERS
SEASIDE RESORTS
MOUNTAIN RESORTS
CITRUS FRUIT
TOBACCO
CASPIAN SEA
TOB
CORN
CITRUS FRUIT
FISH
Frunze
COTTON
SUNFLOWERS
Tashkent
Ashkhabad
TOBACCO

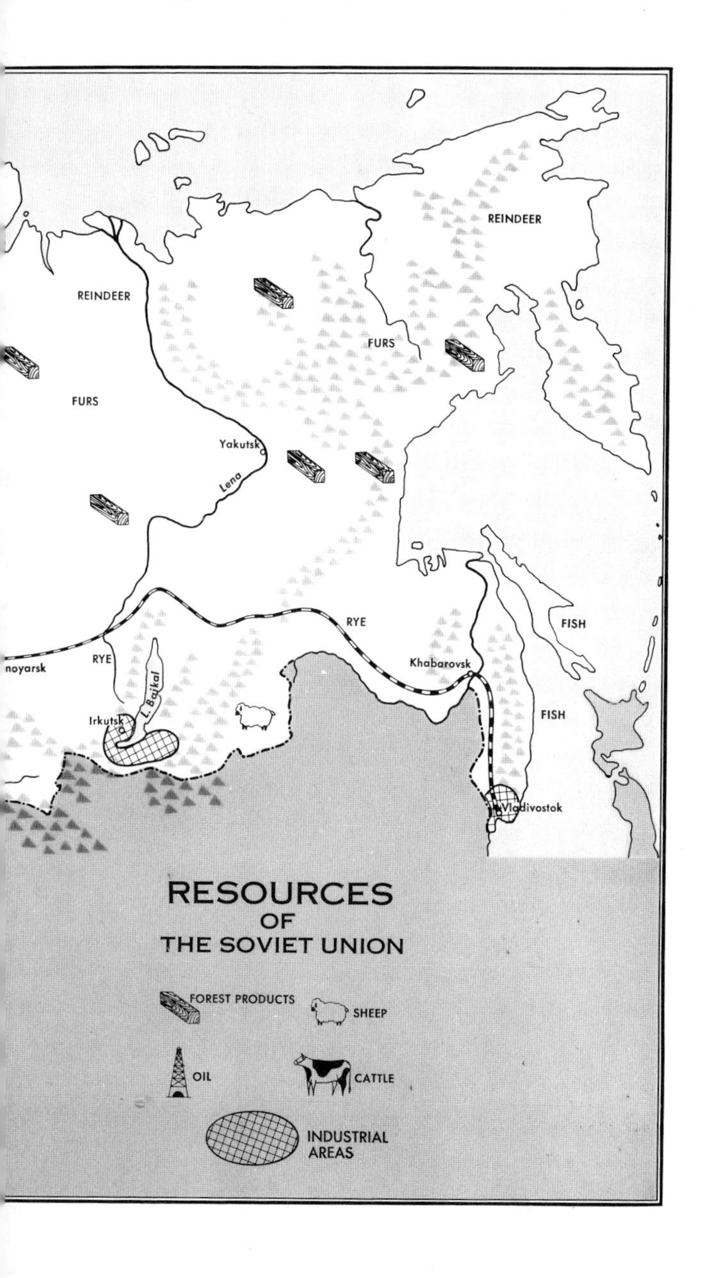
REINDEER
REINDEER
FURS
FURS
Yakutsk
Lena
RYE
RYE
noyarsk
Irkutsk
L. Baikal
Khabarovsk
FISH
FISH
Vladivostok
RESOURCES
OF
THE SOVIET UNION
FOREST PRODUCTS
SHEEP
OIL
CATTLE
INDUSTRIAL
AREAS

ONE

LAND AND PEOPLE

The Soviet Union is a vast country, the largest in the world. Over eight and one-half million square miles in area, it covers one-sixth of the world's inhabited land surface. Straddling the continents of Europe and Asia, the Soviet Union is as large as all of North America. It stretches over 5,000 miles from the Baltic Sea to the Bering Sea (compared with about 3,000 miles from the western to the eastern coasts of the United States) and well over 2,000 miles from the Arctic Ocean to the southern edge of the Caspian Sea (compared with about 1,500 miles from the northern to the southern borders of the United States). The difference in time of day between Moscow and the shores of the Bering Sea is 11 hours (compared with 4 between Florida and California).

Geographically the Soviet Union may be divided into the East European Plain and Siberia. The East European Plain, where 70 percent of the people live, is separated from sparsely settled Siberia by the Ural Mountains. Siberia itself is further divided by the Yenisei River into the West Siberian Plain and the

Central Siberian Plateau and East Siberian highlands. Though the country is bordered by relatively high mountains in the south, the Central Siberian Plateau and the East Siberian highlands are of low and medium height; and the Ural Mountains, which divide Europe from Asia, seldom exceed 6,000 feet. With the enormous plains and the plateau dominating the scene, the general impression of the country is one of flatness.

The change from plains to plateaus to highlands occurs from west to east. The change in vegetation and soil, on the other hand, proceeds from north to south across the continent. In the very north, along the Arctic shore, there is a barren region, called "tundra," whose ground is perennially frozen. South of the tundra there is a broad strip of evergreen forest, called "taiga." Part of it is swampy and so dense as to be practically impassable. The forest floor is marshy, for the soil is ever frozen here, too; and the melted snow cannot be absorbed.

Farther south the evergreens give way to a mixture of cone-bearing and leaf-growing trees. There are spruces and Scots firs, birch trees and aspens, larches, oaks, ashes, and elms. Together, the taiga and the mixed forests cover about half of the entire country. They form the largest forest region on the globe and contain about one-quarter of the world's timber reserves. The soil which nourishes broadleaf trees is generally good for agriculture. Much of this forest area has been cleared, therefore, and is being farmed. It was in the mixed forest zone that the principality of Muscovy developed.

Still farther south is the steppe region. Although it is bare of trees because of insufficient rain, it has rich black soil. It provides about two-thirds of the cultivated land of the Soviet Union and may be regarded as its "grain basket." In the very south are the semidesert and desert soils of Central Asia. As hot winds blow across the dry land of Central Asia, the fields look like seas of ripening grain under the clear blue skies of summer.

The nature of the land and the vegetation influenced the course of history. Early Russians found in the forests not only timber and good earth but also protection from invaders on horseback. The steppe, to which the Russians expanded later, had fertile black soil, but it offered shelter neither from the scorching sun and the icy winds nor from nomadic raiders. The absence of a natural barrier was one factor in the establishment of a strong government to defend the country from foreign attacks. At the same time, the absence of a natural barrier encouraged Russian expansion eastward.

Natural highways led the Russians across the continent. Some of the world's largest rivers and their tributaries and enormous lakes provided a network of transportation. Although the major rivers generally offered north-south routes, many of the tributaries formed an east-west link. Hunters and traders lugged their little boats overland between the water-roads. The Volga, over 2,300 miles in length, is the longest river of Europe. Together with several canal systems, it now connects the Caspian Sea with Moscow and the Baltic and White seas. It handles one-third of Russia's river freight. The Dnieper is Europe's third largest river (the Danube being the second). Like the Don, which flows from the central upland to the Sea of Azov, and the Northern Dvina, which empties into the White Sea, the Dnieper has played an important role in Russian history. Farther east, in Siberia, the Ob, Irtysh, Yenisei, Lena, and Amur rivers are important waterways. The Amur is of particular interest because for much of its course it forms part of the lengthy boundary with China.

The lakes and inland seas of the Soviet Union are impressive and important, too. The Caspian Sea, which the Soviet Union embraces on three sides, is the largest inland sea in the world. It is rich in salmon and sturgeon, from whose eggs Russia's celebrated caviar is prepared. Beautiful Lake Baikal also has an abundance of fish and seals. Almost 400 miles long and nearly 50 miles wide, it is the largest fresh water lake of Eurasia. It is also the deepest fresh water lake on earth.

The Soviet Union is touched by seas, but most of her ports (like her rivers) are frozen part of the year. The desire for year-round outlets to the oceans of the world directed Russian attention to ice-free ports in Korea and South Manchuria in the nineteenth century, adding further "geographic" stimulus to Russian expansion.

The size of the Soviet Union makes generalization difficult. It has many climates. The north, for example, has an arctic climate, with long, cold winters and short, cool summers. The south has a subtropical climate. In-between lies a temperate belt. Temperatures differ not only from north to south but also between west and east. The climate gets severer in the east as the distance from the moderating influence of the Atlantic Ocean increases.

Rainfall like temperature decreases eastward in the Soviet Union, except on the slopes of mountains.

Everybody loves a parade, and the citizens of Leningrad are no exception.

Because there is insufficient rain, agriculture in many areas will remain limited until modern methods of irrigation are introduced. In the steppes north of the Caspian Sea, rainfall measures only a little over 6 inches a year; the western slopes of the Ural Mountains count about 24 inches, and the region of Smolensk, on the Dnieper River, about 25. Central Siberia enjoys somewhat more rainfall than western Siberia, but the total is still under 20 inches. Only along the coast of the mountain-ringed Black Sea is there ample rain, reaching a maximum of almost 100 inches at Batumi.

The labeling of the Soviet Union as the "East" tends to hide the northerly location of the country. Odessa on the Black Sea, along the Soviet Union's southern border, for example, is farther north than the northern boundary of the state of New York. Leningrad, with a population of over 3 million, is the world's northernmost city of its size. It is farther north than Copenhagen (Denmark), Stockholm (Sweden), or even Oslo (Norway); it is farther north than Peking (China) and Juneau (Alaska). Toward the end of May, Leningrad has its so-called "white nights," during which it does not get completely dark at all. As early as November the northeastern portion of European Russia experiences freezing temperatures.

In the worst weather it is so cold that it seems to burn. You launch yourself out of double doors into the street and you gasp. You narrow your shrinking nostrils to give your lungs a chance to get acclimatized, but you gasp again and go on gasping. Ears are well covered against frostbite, but eyebrows and moustache grow icicles in bunches, and sweat runs from under your fur cap and freezes on your temples. Presently a tickle, and the longer hairs of your nostrils have become rigid with ice. Another moment, surely, and the whole nostril will freeze over: in a panic you warm your nose with your glove, but the nostrils do not freeze, and you go on warming your nose and stinging cheeks with your glove, and you go on gasping. Half an hour's walk gives you the exercise of an ordinary afternoon. The only relief is a warm blast from the exhaust of a passing lorry; it is impossible, you think, to bear it all for long, but you can and do. . . .[1]

In northeastern Siberia, in Verkhoyansk, the thermometer has registered as low as −93°F; in Oimyakon, −96°F. Even in southern Siberia temperatures of −40°F are common. The northerly location of the country means a limited amount of land that can be cultivated, and the long winters leave a short growing season—two major handicaps for Soviet agriculture. Russian summers, on the other hand, are mild, except in the hot steppes and deserts of Soviet Central Asia. In Moscow, where the average low temperature in January is about 5°F, the thermometer does not rise to more than an average daily high of 71° in July.

The long winters make summer doubly welcome. Spring brings a thaw into Russian life. In the words of one observer:

Nothing in Russian life is more dramatic than this leap from muffled winter into summer. Life behind double windows is transmuted into life with windows wide open, and out in the sunshine there is a swarming around building sites and over roofs, a hurling away of rusty ironwork, a blossoming of skyblue tramcars, and a coming alive of walls in cream and pink and buff and grey and green.[2]

The Soviet Union has a population of almost 230 million—more inhabitants than any other country, except China and India. One out of every 14 persons on earth lives in the U.S.S.R. In America we often speak of the entire country as "Russia" and of its people as "the Russians." In the Soviet Union, on the other hand, people talk primarily of the "Soiuz" or "Union" and of themselves as "Soviet" citizens. "Russian" is the name reserved for those of eastern Slavic background and culture, especially the so-called Great Russians, who inhabit primarily the north and center of European Russia. Armenians, Georgians, Jews, and other national minorities are not allowed to classify themselves as "Russian" on their identification cards.

The name U.S.S.R. ("CCCP" as it appears in the Russian alphabet) dates back to 1922. It is the official name of the Soviet Union and stands for "Union of Soviet Socialist Republics," a term which gives no preference to any nationality. As the Russian Empire expanded over the centuries, territories inhabited by peoples of different races and cultures, speaking various languages, were annexed. The fifteen union republics which constitute the Soviet Union represent the major nationalities of the Russian state. The Russian Soviet Federated Socialist Republic, where most people of Russian stock live, is the largest republic; it occupies about three-fourths of the territory of the Soviet Union. The Georgian Soviet Socialist Republic is inhabited primarily by Georgians, the Armenian Soviet Socialist Republic by Armenians, the Uzbek Soviet Socialist Republic by Uzbeks, and so forth. Smaller minorities form "autonomous regions," and still smaller ones form "national districts." In theory every republic and thus every major nationality is self-governing. Yet, while the minorities are free to develop their own cultures, they are not free

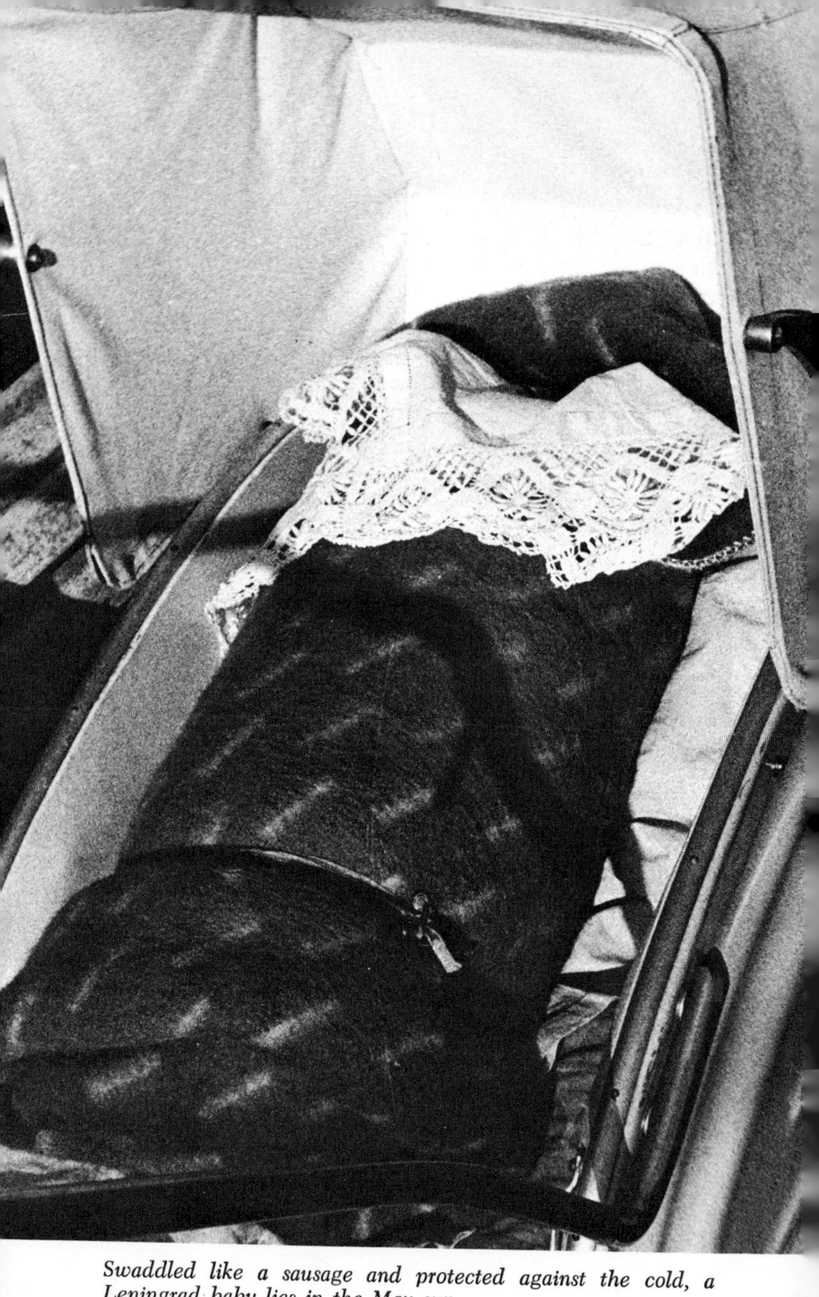

Swaddled like a sausage and protected against the cold, a Leningrad baby lies in the May sun.

to determine their own form of government. They are denied full religious expression, tribal self-rule, and independent parties. Like the Russians themselves, they are subjects of a centralized, totalitarian state.

The Russians belong to the eastern branch of the Slavic family, a large group of people speaking a Slavic tongue. The Slavic languages, like English, are part of the Indo-European language group. Russian is written in the Slavic or "Cyrillic" alphabet. Named after its developer, the Greek missionary Cyril, the alphabet contains a number of letters that are similar to or identical with Greek (Г, А, Ф, Λ, П, Х). The Russians are also called the Great Russians, to distinguish them from the closely related Ukrainians (once known as Little Russians) and the Byelorussians. Generally fair-haired and on the average somewhat shorter than Americans, the Great Russians are descendants of the northern and eastern tribes of early Russia. They number over 115 million—about half the population of the Soviet Union.

The Ukrainians are also eastern Slavs, but they are descended from the tribes which lived in the southern portion of Russia. They number about 37 million, or about 15 percent of the total population. Separated from the rest of the country by Lithuanian and Polish conquests in the fourteenth, fifteenth, and sixteenth centuries, the Ukrainians began to develop a national identity of their own. In the nineteenth century some began calling themselves Ukrainians, after the Little-Russian Ukraine, a state of the seventeenth century. They are generally blond. Their language is somewhat different from, but closely related to, Russian. They live not only in the Ukraine but in other parts of the Soviet Union as well. The Byelorussians also are eastern Slavs. They number close to 8 million, or about 5 percent of the total population. In language, religion, and appearance they resemble the Great Russians and the Ukrainians. Together these three Slavic groups make up more than two-thirds of the total population of the Soviet Union.

The non-Slavic peoples who inhabit the various union republics are of different racial and cultural backgrounds. About 8 percent are Turkic-speaking Muslims—Turkmens, Uzbeks, Kazaks, Kirghiz, and Azers—whose lands were annexed by Russia in the nineteenth century. Traditionally the Muslims believe in one God, Allah, and in Muhammad, his chief prophet. The name of their religion, Islam, means "submission" to God's will. But today in the Soviet Union Islam, like Christianity, has lost most of its influence. The Turkmens have retained their tribal and clan divisions. Raising sheep and horses and busy with cotton cultivation, silk, and carpet weaving, they live primarily in the oases of Turkmenia, the southernmost republic of the U.S.S.R. The Uzbeks, who took part in the Mongol conquest of Russia, have Mongoloid features from intermarriage with the Mongols. Inhabiting Uzbekistan, which is part of the region once called Turkistan, they have been a peace-loving, hospitable people for many centuries. They raise sheep and produce cotton and silk. The Kazaks, in addition to raising livestock, are engaged in crop cultivation. The Kirghiz also have Mongoloid features. Their republic of Kirghizia, like the Tadzhik and Kazak republics, touches the Chinese border. The

Azers are a mixture of Caucasian and Iranian-speaking people who were once subjected to the influence of the Seljuk Turks.

Other nationalities, which have their own union republics, are the Tadzhiks, the Moldavians, the Armenians, the Georgians, the Estonians, the Latvians, and the Lithuanians. The Tadzhiks, like the Turkmens and the Uzbeks, were a Muslim people, conquered in the 1880's. They speak an Iranian language. The Moldavians are a Latin-speaking people, related to the Rumanians. They are Orthodox Christian in

Huge chunks of ice are floating down the Neva River (out of camera range), but with the arrival of spring, Leningraders peel off their outerwear and soak up the sun along the walls of the Fortress of Peter and Paul.

background and are principally farmers. The Armenians, too, are an ancient Christian people, belonging originally to the Armenian Gregorian Church, and speak an Indo-European language. Very active in trade and industry, less than half of the Soviet Union's more than three and one-half million Armenians live in Armenia. One-third live in the Russian Republic. The Georgians are a Caucasian-speaking people, once predominately Orthodox Christian in faith. Like the Armenians, they have played an important role in modern Russian history. The Estonians speak a Finnic language; they are predominantly Lutheran in background. The Latvians, too, are largely Lutheran in background, while the Lithuanians are Roman Catholic in heritage. Their languages, Lettish and Lithuanian, belong to the Indo-European family.

In addition to the nationalities which have their own union republics, there are many others, including the Tatars, the Poles, and the Germans. Living in the Volga and Ural areas as well as in western Siberia, the Tatars are among the best educated and most important of the Turkic-speaking Muslim people of the Soviet Union. The Jews, too, are regarded as a national minority in the Soviet Union.

Although in theory all Soviet citizens are "equal," the Russians have remained "more equal" than other nationalities. The majority of Soviet leaders have been Russian, and the top military and government officials, as well as the leading scientists and educators, are mainly Russian. In some ways this is not surprising, because the Russians greatly outnumber the other nationalities. Their predominance is not merely a result of their numbers, however. The U.S.S.R., like the old empire, is primarily a Russian creation, the other peoples and their territories having been added to the Russian Republic after 1922.

During World War II the Soviet Union lost about 20 million people. If one adds to this the number of babies that would probably have been born had there been no war, the population loss amounted to about 40 million. This figure was offset in part by the 20 million people added through annexation of border territory. There are generally more women than men in the Soviet Union, a fact which explains to some extent why women must share in doing heavy work.

From the 1930's to the 1950's many people migrated from rural to urban areas. The old cities grew rapidly and new ones sprang up. Today the population of the Soviet Union is increasing more gradually. The population center has been shifting eastward, with Siberia gaining inhabitants at a faster rate than European Russia.

TWO

HISTORY: IMPERIAL RUSSIA

The history of ancient Russia is cloaked in legend and controversy. Only beginning with the tenth century do we get a relatively clear picture of the country. It was not yet Russia, in the sense of a centralized state, but a federation of city-states dominated by Kiev.

The city-state of Kiev straddled the trade route from the Scandinavian peninsula to Constantinople, and Kievan Russia as a whole stretched from the Baltic Sea toward the Black Sea. The Kievan princes, who according to tradition were Norsemen in origin, fought back hostile nomadic peoples and extended their rule over nearby Slavic tribes. They clashed and traded with the Arabic East and the Byzantine (Eastern Roman) Empire.

In the tenth century Kievan Russia was converted to Christianity. Since the gospel reached them by way of Constantinople rather than Rome, the Russians became Orthodox (Greek Catholic) and not Roman

Catholic like most Europeans. Byzantine influence was not confined to religion. Russian art, concepts of government, and diplomatic forms were given an "eastern" touch. The Byzantine influence differed in various aspects of life. In government, for example, it contributed to the joining of state and church. In language, it led to the adoption of the Cyrillic alphabet.

By the eleventh century, Kievan Russia had attained some political unity, as well as cultural and economic prosperity. One foreign merchant was so impressed by the splendor of the buildings and the variety of products that were available that he called Kiev the rival of Constantinople. In the second half of the twelfth century, however, the decline of the Byzantine trade, the basis of Kiev's original strength, weakened her position. The attacks of nomadic tribes and rivalry among her own princes resulted in the eventual break-up of Kievan Russia.

The country split into a number of territories. Some were eventually annexed by Poland and Lithuania; others joined together to form the Grand Duchy of Vladimir, which carried on the Kievan tradition. The collapse of central authority increased the importance of local noblemen (boyars), on whom the populace became dependent for protection and government. Without a strong central government the country lay exposed to foreign invasion; and some of Kiev's inhabitants migrated to other regions, particularly to the northeast.

Like the Poles and Lithuanians, Swedes, Danes, and German Teutonic Knights threatened the Russian lands. But it was the Mongols and their Tatar subjects, attacking from the east, who conquered the

Russians. The Mongols overran the country in the thirteenth century, making it part of an empire that embraced most of the Eurasian continent, including China. Later Russians were to regard themselves as the legitimate heirs to the possessions of both the Byzantine and Mongol empires, the two-headed Russian eagle (the national emblem until 1917) facing in both directions. But this does not mean that the Russians became Tatars at heart. They tried hard to escape direct Mongol rule either by accepting Mongol demands for tribute or by resisting them. Indeed, the Russians like to look upon themselves as the shield which protected Europe from Mongol conquest.

As the Mongols began to quarrel among themselves, the Russian princes gradually reasserted their authority. In the fifteenth century, when Mongol power had visibly declined, they threw off the "Tatar yoke." The leading opponent of the Mongols was the principality of Muscovy, which had become important economically and politically because of the strategic position of the city of Moscow and the ability of its rulers. It was Grand Duke Ivan III of Muscovy (also known as Ivan the Great) who put an end to Mongol domination in 1480 when he refused to pay any further tribute to them. Once he had strengthened Muscovy, unified a number of Russian lands, and begun the formation of a central government, Ivan III assumed the title of "Tsar," the Russian equivalent of "Caesar." It is from this point (the end of the fifteenth century) that we can properly speak of "Russia."

In the middle of the sixteenth century Ivan IV, the grandson of Ivan III, further extended the authority of the central government. Russia became an autocracy—a country ruled by an autocrat or individual

These beacons, which once guided ships into St. Petersburg, now are lit only on holidays and special occasions.

with unlimited power. In the process not only the nobles but also the people were deprived of whatever independence they had. The contributions of Ivan IV to the centralization of Russia's government and to the expansion of her borders were overshadowed by his fear of disloyalty. He had thousands of his countrymen tortured to death and even killed one of his own sons in a fit of insane temper. He is known in history, therefore, as "Ivan the Dread" or "Ivan the Terrible."

At the beginning of the seventeenth century the Russian Empire was threatened by revolutionary upheaval, civil wars, and Polish invasion. It survived, and the dynasty begun by Michael Romanov, when he was elected to the throne in 1613, was to last until 1917.

Although Michael Romanov had been elected to the throne by an assembly of delegates from the provinces, his successors inherited the throne. Peter I (Peter the Great) restored, indeed further developed, autocratic government. Ruling with firmness and imagination, he sought to modernize Russia, particularly Russian technology, along European lines. He had visited Western Europe to observe its methods firsthand. With a modernized army and a newly built navy he defeated the Swedes and gained possession of several Baltic Sea ports. These became commercial and cultural "windows" upon Europe and significantly influenced Russian development.

Peter the Great transferred the capital from Moscow to St. Petersburg, a city newly built by him and named after his patron saint (1703). Situated on the Neva River, which empties into the Gulf of Finland, St. Petersburg (now called Leningrad) faced westward. Its back turned toward the ancient traditions of Moscow, St. Petersburg stood as a symbol of Europeanization. Yet Russia retained her interest in the east. By the middle of the seventeenth century Russian explorers had reached the Pacific Ocean; and in 1689 Russia concluded a treaty with China, a century and a half before Great Britain and the United States did so. The possibilities of trade with Japan, the Philippines, and America, as well as with China, interested Peter the Great.

After the death of Peter the Great, the pace of Europeanization slowed down. It was accelerated again in the latter part of the eighteenth century by Catherine the Great. Catherine was a German princess who ascended the throne following the overthrow and murder of her pro-Prussian husband Peter III by the court nobility (apparently with her knowledge). One of the "Enlightened Rulers" of Europe, Catherine patterned her court life after the splendor of Versailles under Louis XIV. She was a patron of the arts and encouraged Russian and foreign actors, dancers, and writers—even those with whose ideas she disagreed. The French Revolution and the execution of Louis XVI frightened Catherine (as it did other monarchs), and she lost her liberal enthusiasms. But she remained true to the policy of Westernization and involved Russia increasingly in the affairs of Europe, extending the borders of the empire at the expense of other states. Thus, for example, Russia joined Austria and Prussia in dividing up Poland.

The year that Paul I succeeded Catherine (1796), Napoleon launched France on a policy of expansion. Paul I joined England, Holland, and Austria in opposition to Napoleon. But the very excellence of the Russian armies, which, like the navy, had been further modernized under Paul, aroused the fears of the allies. Deserted by them on the field of battle, the Russians sought to improve relations with France. When Paul was murdered in 1801, his son, Alexander I, became Tsar. Alexander tried military measures and diplomacy to keep Napoleon away from his borders, but in 1812 the French invaded Russia. The Russian armies withdrew, "scorching the earth" by burning whatever shelter or food the enemy might need. In this way they lost territory but gained time. They succeeded in exhausting the French forces and though they lost Moscow, they saved their country and finally defeated Napoleon. Russia thus gained great influence in Europe. At the Congress of Vienna in 1815 it played a leading role. The Holy Alliance, which was an agreement of the Christian monarchs to make the world safe for autocracy, was in part the creation of Alexander I.

But young Russian officers who were stationed in France following the defeat of Napoleon were exposed to the ideas of the French Revolution. Upon their return home, they conspired to attain political, social, and economic reforms. Taking advantage of the confusion that followed the death of Alexander, who had no heir, when it was not clear which of his brothers would succeed to the throne, the young revolutionaries instigated a mutiny among some of the troops in St. Petersburg. They marched forth demanding "Constantine [the brother they preferred] and a Constitution." Their demonstration, in December of 1825, failed to trigger a general uprising, as they had hoped. The revolt was crushed, the main leaders hanged, and over a hundred young noble officers were sentenced to prison or exiled. But the Decembrists—as the participants in the December uprising came to be called—were not forgotten. Their example inspired Russia's growing liberal and revolutionary movement.

On the other hand, Nicholas I, the brother against whom the demonstration had been directed and who succeeded to the throne, became the more confirmed in his opposition to representative government and freedom of expression. He regarded himself as an absolute ruler by divine right. In his determination to stamp out political subversion and to impose loyalty and conformity on all his subjects, Nicholas neglected the economic ills that plagued Russian society.

Serfdom, which was not unique to Russia, persisted in that country longer than in Western Europe. It imposed a crushing burden not only on the serfs, who with their families formed the larger part of the population, but on the economy as a whole. The serfs were unskilled workers who lived in poverty in spite of backbreaking labor; they could be sold and needed their master's permission to marry. Consequently they were dissatisfied, inefficient, and unproductive. Serfdom held back Russian agriculture; it delayed the growth of commerce, towns, and industry. The backwardness of the Russian system was exposed when Russia, whose armies had excited the jealousy of some of its allies at the time of Napoleon, was defeated in the Crimean War (1854-1855) by France, England, the Ottoman Empire, and Sardinia.

Alexander II, who succeeded Nicholas in 1855, realized that drastic changes were necessary if Russia were to keep pace with other countries, indeed if it wished to forestall revolution at home. Writers who depicted the wretched living conditions of the masses smoothed his path, and in 1861 his Emancipation Proclamation wiped out serfdom and the ancient privileges of the landlords. Although Alexander's promise of legal equality was not fulfilled and the peasants did not achieve complete freedom or economic well-being, the basis of the old social order was swept away.

Alexander, the "Tsar Liberator" as he was known henceforth, initiated many reforms. He modernized the financial system (including tax collection), furthered education, established open jury trials, and granted some local self-government. His efforts were cut short, however, when a terrorist's bomb took his life in 1881.

Shocked by the violent death of his father, Alexander III reversed the trend toward liberalization and during the years of his reign (1881-1894) sought to maintain the autocracy of old. So did his son, Nicholas II (1894-1917), a man of indecisive personality whose strong and increasingly mystical German wife urged him not to weaken the principle of absolutism, whereby all authority rested solely in him. The revolutionary movement could not be halted by repression alone, however. On the contrary, it gained momentum. Industrialization, which began in the late nineteenth century, did not solve the country's economic and social problems. Though it developed slowly in comparison with the industrialization of Western Europe, it came too fast for Russians to adjust to it.

Russian intellectuals, unlike those in Western Europe who identified themselves with the middle classes, were deeply interested in socialism, an economic doctrine that opposed private property and

Moscow children admire the enormous sixteenth-century gun, popularly known as "Tsar-cannon," in the Kremlin grounds.

advocated its use for the welfare of the public. Around the middle of the nineteenth century men like Alexander Herzen were attracted by French socialism, which sought to set up "utopian" or ideal societies. Some intellectuals in the 1860's and 1870's tried to bring on a popular revolution by the violent action of a few individuals; they thought that the assassination of the Tsar or his ministers would stir the people to a mass uprising. Others went to the villages to educate the peasants in the hope of laying the foundations for an agrarian socialist society. But with the spread of science and industry in the latter part of the nineteenth century, the feeling grew that only united action on a large scale could topple the old regime, and many intellectuals turned to "Scientific Socialism" or Marxism.

Marxism is a political and social system based on the philosophical writings of two nineteenth-century Germans: Karl Marx and Friedrich Engels. They, in turn, had been influenced by Western, notably German, philosophers before them, in particular by Georg Hegel. Hegel conceived of the universe as a single whole, in which all parts are related to each other. The Marxists accepted Hegel's position that the progress of history is "dialectical," that is to say, that history moves forward like an intelligent dialogue, in which the clash of opposite views leads to a blend of understanding. They rejected Hegel's "idealism," his notion that institutions and objects essentially represent ideas, and his view that the state fulfills a divine purpose. They argued that only matter exists and that material considerations, therefore, motivate man. His religion, culture, and political system are by-products of his economic setup. Combining this materialist view with the dialectic form of change, Marx and Engels evolved the concept of "dialectical materialism."

In history, according to the Marxists, the clash of opposites is expressed in the class struggle between the exploiters (the owners of the means of production such as factories) and the exploited (those who live by their labor). At various stages in history there were different classes of exploiters and exploited. By the nineteenth century the owners of the means of production, known as "capitalists," were arrayed against the propertyless urban workers, the "proletariat." Marx predicted that the capitalists eventually would drive each other out of business and, greatly reduced in number, would be deprived of their spoils by the working class. Marx did not argue that this should happen because it was fair or right; he predicted that it was bound to happen as a matter of historical development.

Marxists disagreed on the methods and speed with which the old order was to be transformed. Many favored a gradual, relatively peaceful change. But it was the much more extreme faction, the Bolshevik or Communist movement under the leadership of Lenin, which ultimately was to reshape Russia.

In 1904-1905 Russia was defeated by Japan, whose ambitions on the Asian continent clashed with its own. The humiliating reverses that Russia suffered in the Russo-Japanese War discredited the Tsarist regime further in the eyes of the public. A general clamor for reforms spread throughout the land in 1905, and revolutionary leaders took advantage of popular dissatisfaction and the weakness of the imperial government to call for a general strike. So successful and complete was the general strike, that Tsar

Nicholas II was forced to issue the October Manifesto, which guaranteed such basic civil liberties as freedom of speech, freedom of conscience, and freedom of assembly. It also provided for the approval of all laws by a newly established parliament, called the Duma. Thus the Revolution of 1905, as the turbulent events of the year came to be known, modified the absolute monarchy of the Romanovs to some extent.

The Duma did not govern the nation. In part this was because Nicholas did not live up to his promises once the war against Japan had been concluded and the armies brought back. The liberal leaders, furthermore, failed to obtain popular support and lacked the unity and political experience necessary for constitutional government. When the members of the bourgeoisie (the middle class) and of the intelligentsia (the educated) did not succeed in making Nicholas live up to his promises and gradually lost their revolutionary zeal, they forfeited leadership. When revolution broke out again in 1917, in the midst of World War I, the proletariat and eventually the peasantry turned against the bourgeoisie and the intelligentsia as well as against the Tsarist regime.

THREE

HISTORY: COMMUNIST RUSSIA

The Communists did not overthrow the Russian monarchy. No political group really did. The Tsarist government collapsed from lack of support when the burdens of World War I proved too heavy for its shaky foundation, undermined by corruption and lack of vision. Neither the masses nor the intelligentsia—not even the monarchists—rallied to its assistance when hungry rioters in the capital of Petrograd (formerly St. Petersburg) brought on a national upheaval. The February Revolution of 1917—so called because it took place in February according to the old Russian calendar, in March according to present reckoning—occurred with the approval of most Russians.

There was little bloodshed. Within three days, three centuries of Romanov rule were ended. Nicholas II abdicated in favor of his brother, Grand Duke Michael; and when Michael refused the crown, the reins of government passed into the hands of the Provisional Government, hastily formed from members of the Duma.

The leaders of the Provisional Government were conservatives and liberals—they wanted moderate and gradual reforms. The problems that faced the Provisional Government were many. Three deserve special attention: the war, the government's limited authority, and the impatience and radicalism of the masses. Although the war was obviously very unpopular, Alexander Kerensky, who succeeded Prince George Lvov as Prime Minister in July, believed that it was the sacred obligation of Russia not to desert her allies. Noble as this may have been in theory, it proved fatal in fact, since the Communist slogan of "peace and bread" rang louder than the government's appeals to patriotism and honor.

Side by side with the Provisional Government there had come into being in the capital a Soviet (Council) of Workers' and Soldiers' Deputies. This Soviet and similar Soviets that sprang up all over Russia, as well as the All-Russian Congress of Soviets which convened in June, were more representative of the masses than was the Provisional Government. Their actions competed with those of the Provisional Government and hampered the execution of its policies.

Communist (originally called Bolshevik) revolutionaries were more radical than the members of the Provisional Government. They called for the overthrow of the "middle class" Provisional Government and for the surrender of all power to the Soviets. "War to the palaces, peace to the huts!" they proclaimed. The reluctance of the Provisional Government to suppress by force both Communist revolutionaries and generals who were loyal to the old system or wanted a military dictatorship (for that, it seemed to the liberals, would have been to act no better than the old regime) left the field to the extremists. By the time the government realized that stern measures were necessary to preserve the budding democracy, it was too late. On November 7, 1917, the Communists overthrew the Provisional Government. As the date, according to the old calendar (in use up to February, 1918), was October 25, the Communist Revolution is known as the October Revolution.

Like the Tsarist regime before it, the Provisional Government fell practically without resistance. Before long, however, the Communists were confronted by a so-called "Counterrevolution." The "Whites" who opposed the "Reds" (Communists) in the civil war that began in the summer of 1918 and lasted until the end of 1920 included the most diverse elements—army officers, middle-class intellectuals, secondary school students, and workers—with vastly different political views. United only by anticommunism, they found it difficult to consolidate their efforts. Successful at first, the Whites could not sustain their drive. Geographically scattered, outnumbered, and inadequately supplied, the White movement went down in defeat.

During the civil war English, French, Japanese, and American troops were dispatched to Russia, primarily to seaports in the north and in the far east. The Allies (but not Russia) were still at war with Germany, and the purpose of the Allied intervention originally was to prevent the enemy from seizing the vast stores of military supplies at these ports. Upon the defeat of Germany, Allied aims were modified. A Czechoslovak legion, formed by the Provisional

The Soviet star atop the Kremlin towers marks the transfer of the seat of government by the Communists from St. Petersburg, or Petrograd, back to Moscow.

Government, was assisted in leaving the country. Japanese troops occupied Sakhalin Island and moved into Siberia in large numbers in the hope of separating the region east of Lake Baikal from Russia as an independent buffer state, if not as a colony of Japan. The United States participated in the Allied intervention partly as a check on Japanese expansion. France and England occupied regions in southern Russia, in whose coal, iron, and oil resources they were interested. The general desire to halt the spread of communism also was a factor in the intervention; but except for some Japanese action in Siberia and for Czechoslovak efforts to fight their way out of the country, the Allies did not directly participate in the civil war. They gave some financial and material support to the White forces, but not enough to affect the outcome of the struggle. The bulk of the Allied troops, which had been landed in 1918, were withdrawn the following year. Only the Japanese remained in Siberia until 1922, and on Sakhalin Island until 1925. Ineffectual as the intervention had been, however, it had been viewed as a real threat by the Communists and had intensified Communist hostility and mistrust of the West.

The victory of the Communists in the civil war was due in large measure to the dynamic leadership of Lenin, whose original name had been Vladimir Ilyich Ulyanov. The son of a provincial school inspector, he had been engaged in political activity from boyhood. Lenin was greatly affected at the age of seventeen by the execution of his eldest brother, who had been involved in an attempt on the life of Alexander III. After studying Marxism, he was expelled from the University of Kazan for his part in a student

cholera."[4] Yet scientific as Marxism claims to be, it is based on faith, for the past cannot be projected into the future with any certainty; and Marx's version of a classless society that would ultimately emerge out of the class struggle could be believed but not proven.

Dogmatic adherence to Marxist-Leninist principles, it should be added, does not restrict Communist leaders to a certain set of actions. On the grounds that the end justifies the means, they pursue whatever policies seem best suited at the moment to further their cause. In other words, while the overall strategy remains fairly constant, the tactics are changed as the situation demands.

The government that the Communists set up when they seized power in November, 1917, known as the Council of People's Commissars, was formed in the midst of war. Its harsh policies, as it struggled desperately to survive against foreign and domestic foes, were labeled "War Communism." Industries were "nationalized" (taken over by the national government), as was the land. Although the peasants continued to till the land, they were forced to surrender to the state practically all they raised. Private commerce was abolished, and the government took over the distribution of food and goods. Opposition to these steps, particularly by the peasants, was ruthlessly crushed.

The Communists sacrificed a large slice of the former Russian Empire in Europe when they made a separate treaty of peace with Germany, the Treaty of Brest-Litovsk, in March, 1918. It proclaimed the independence from Russia of Poland, Latvia, Lithuania, Estonia, Finland, and the Ukraine and ceded a portion of Transcaucasia to Turkey. When the Allies de-

Change of guards at the mausoleum. For a while Stalin's body lay side by side with that of Lenin; the embalmed corpse and the name above the entrance were removed during the "de-Stalinization" drive.

feated the Central Powers, the Communists tried to nullify these provisions. Though they failed to block the formation of Poland, Latvia, Lithuania, Estonia, and Finland, they retained most of the Ukraine and successfully prevented the non-Russian peoples of the Transcaucasus from seceding.

In July of 1918 the Communists founded the Russian Soviet Federated Socialist Republic. Four years later, they transformed it into the Union of Soviet Socialist Republics. Theoretically a federation of Russia, Byelorussia, the Ukraine, Transcaucasia, and later additional union republics, the U.S.S.R. was a highly centralized state with all power in the hands of the Communist leaders.

In contrast to the October Revolution, which had been almost bloodless, the years of the civil war (1918-1920) were crowded with fighting, political executions, epidemics, droughts, and famine, which claimed the lives of some 20 million people. Although victorious politically, the Communists faced economic ruin and internal rebellions. After the defeat of the White forces, therefore, the Soviet leaders, on Lenin's insistence, moved from "War Communism" to the "New Economic Policy" (1921).

The New Economic Policy (NEP) did not mean a change in objective. The goal of socialism was not abandoned. The NEP was a temporary retreat for a new advance. It rectified some of the excesses of "War Communism" by a compromise designed to bring workers and peasants closer together and increase production. It allowed greater economic freedom within the framework of socialism; there was no relaxation in political control. The produce of the peasants was no longer taken by the government.

They paid taxes in produce but were free to sell the rest of their products as they chose. Forced labor was stopped, industry was decentralized (rearranged under independent trusts or occasionally leased to individuals), and much of distribution was returned to private hands. But public utilities and major industries remained state operated.

The new system—Lenin called it "state capitalism"—was remarkably effective. By 1928 industry reached the level of production it had had before World War I, and in agriculture the old area of cultivation was even exceeded. But the appearance of a large number of small businessmen and of prosperous peasants (the kulaks) threatened to undermine the social foundations of the Soviet state, for both groups clung to private property and the kulaks resisted government policy to merge the land that they tilled into collective farms.

There were Communists who wished to continue the New Economic Policy on the ground that the world revolution, which they believed must occur before socialism could succeed in Russia, was not yet in sight. Others countered that a socialist system could be established and preserved in Russia, even in the midst of a hostile world; they advocated the building of a socialist state in Russia as a springboard for world revolution. It was this position that carried the greatest appeal for most Communists and helped its advocate, Joseph Stalin, to seize the reins of government after Lenin's death.

The power struggle that ensued in 1922, when Lenin suffered a stroke, and intensified after his death in 1924 was not decided by the ballot box. Leon Trotsky, a dynamic intellectual and brilliant organizer who had been Lenin's most able associate during the October Revolution and persistently advocated world revolution, greatly exceeded Stalin and other rivals in intellect and prestige. But Stalin skillfully played the various contenders against each other and used his position as general secretary of the Communist party to build up a political machine that overcame all opposition. In 1927 the All-Union Congress of the Communist party acknowledged him as the leader of the party. With his rivals silenced or crushed—Trotsky was exiled to Mexico, where he was later assassinated —Stalin ruled the Soviet Union as absolute dictator from 1928 to 1953.

Joseph Stalin was not a Russian by nationality. He was a native of Georgia in the Transcaucasus and retained a Georgian accent throughout his life. The son of a shoemaker, he had gone to a church school and a theological seminary, from which he had been expelled. He engaged in revolutionary activities, primarily in the Caucasus, and rallied to Lenin's side in 1917. Crude but shrewd, hard headed, and strong in organizational ability, Stalin (like Ivan the Terrible) eventually reached the point of madness in his fear of conspiracy and ruthlessly purged real and imaginary foes, including high Communist party leaders and army officers.

Determined to make the Soviet Union a strong, socialist state, Stalin embarked on a series of five-year plans for the development of the national economy. Under these programs individual peasant holdings were joined together or "collectivized"; heavy industry was expanded; and efforts were made to increase productivity and lower prices. Without experience in such unprecedented and complex planning, the vast

Communist bureaucracy that came into being made numerous mistakes and experienced many failures. Although they succeeded in collectivizing agriculture and in making the Soviet Union a great industrial and military power in a relatively short time, the Communists did so at enormous cost to the people.

Groups that opposed collectivization, such as the prosperous peasants, were wiped out; millions of people were sentenced to forced labor on large construction projects and in Siberia; and the population at large was forced to toil long hours at low pay. Consumer goods and public housing were neglected, and living conditions in the Soviet Union remained woefully poor. Considering Russia's resources, the plans laid before World War I, and the passage of time with its general technological progress, it is possible that another form of government in Russia might have achieved industrialization somewhat more slowly but with less hardship.

In 1941 Nazi Germany invaded the Soviet Union. The German armies penetrated deep into Russian territory but were unable to subdue the country. Leningrad (the St. Petersburg of old) heroically withstood a German siege for two and a half years, refusing to surrender even though fighting, starvation, and disease claimed a million and a half of its 4 million residents. At Stalingrad (now Volgagrad) and elsewhere the Russians fought hard with equal determination until their native soil had been freed of the invader.

It is interesting to note that early German successes were aided by lack of Russian opposition. Looking upon the Germans as liberators from the Communist tyranny, many Soviet citizens did not fight; and when the war was over, many who had been moved by the Germans out of Russia refused to go back. But any hopes that the Germans had come as liberators were soon dispelled by Nazi atrocities, and Russian resistance stiffened. Whether the people had been inspired primarily by loyalty to the government, by patriotism, or by hatred of the Germans is less significant, however, than the fact that the Communist regime survived the Great Fatherland War, as it labeled the gigantic conflict.

As in its civil war, Russia lost some 20 million people, and much of its land lay devastated. The task of reconstruction following World War II was enormous, and the living conditions of the people remained pitiful. But renewed patriotism and pride in their victorious armed forces filled the Russian people. At the same time the prestige and influence of the Soviet Union rose sharply throughout Europe and Asia, as Red agents and armies took advantage of the collapse of Germany and Japan and the exhaustion of the Allies. Some countries which had once belonged to the Russian Empire, such as Latvia, Lithuania, and Estonia, had been annexed in 1940. Others, like Czechoslovakia and Hungary, were reduced to "satellites" as Soviet armies, which had occupied them during the war, helped set up Communist governments which would follow Moscow's lead.

After World War II Stalin continued his dictatorial control. Any opposition to his policies was suppressed by the secret police. When he died in 1953, a struggle for control ensued within the Communist party. First George Malenkov, then Nicholas Bulganin and Nikita Khrushchev, and then Khrushchev alone, as head of both the party and the state, emerged at the top. Khrushchev promised greater freedom to the

Soviet people, and though he himself tried to consolidate as much authority as possible in his own hands, he never attained the absolute power of Stalin. His public clowning abroad and his folksy speeches at home (in contrast to the stern and dry manner of Stalin) gave a more human image of Soviet rule. His efforts to provide better housing, clothing, and food for the populace certainly were a great improvement over Stalin's rule. In February, 1956, Khrushchev publicly denounced some of Stalin's crimes and initiated a policy of "de-Stalinization" which led to some relaxation of arbitrary controls over the people. The late dictator's body was removed from the mausoleum on Red Square (where it had lain alongside Lenin), and some of his supporters were dismissed from office.

The de-Stalinization which followed Khrushchev's denunciation of the late dictator divided the Communist camp. China and Albania, for example, objected strongly. At the same time the relaxation of some dictatorial controls spread to the satellite countries and eroded Russian domination. While Khrushchev had accused Stalin of one-man rule, he himself began to act ever-more independently. Moreover, to some Communists he appeared to be impetuous and reckless–banging his shoe on the table at the United Nations and placing Soviet missiles in Cuba. Russia's weakening position, the loss of face over Cuba, the failure of the agricultural program, and other factors undermined Khrushchev's position; and in October, 1964, he was removed from office.

In place of one leader to hold the position of both premier and party secretary, as Lenin, Stalin, and Khrushchev had done, there now were two men. Leonid Brezhnev took over as party secretary, Alexei

Kosygin as premier. Unlike their predecessors who had been active in the Revolution, the new leaders had risen through the party ranks after 1928. They were bureaucrats and, for the time being at least, seemed content to let the organization run things.

In an attempt to gain public acceptance, Brezhnev and Kosygin continued Khrushchev's policy of allowing some loosening-up of Soviet society. Large-scale housing projects and steadily improving consumer goods began to change the appearance of the cities and their inhabitants. But the transformation was merely external; the basic nature of the regime remained almost unchanged.

FOUR

THE SOVIET ECONOMY

Space exploration and missile power dramatize the fact that the Soviet Union is capable of impressive achievements in science and technology. Historically this is a fairly recent development. The civil war had destroyed the greater part of Russian industry, and the first years of Soviet rule were confined to reconstruction. When the Tsarist level of industrial development was regained in 1928, the Soviet economy was still heavily agricultural.

The five-year plans, mentioned in the preceding chapter, boosted Soviet production of machinery, metals, fuels, and chemicals rapidly and substantially in the period from 1928 to 1940. But the Second World War inflicted terrible damage on the Soviet economy. Bitter fighting with the German invaders took place in the heartland of Russian industry and agriculture, and the richest regions of the Soviet Union were laid waste. About a third of Soviet industry was destroyed.

Following the war the Russians began to rebuild their industry with redoubled effort. Soviet seizure of machinery and raw materials in Manchuria, East Germany, and other regions occupied by the Red army helped, but the main burden fell again on the Russian people, as Stalin imposed back-breaking working conditions. By 1953 Soviet industry exceeded the prewar level, though agricultural production remained low and the standard of living poor.

Stalin's successors made many changes. Malenkov, Khrushchev, and Brezhnev paid greater heed to agriculture and assigned more funds to the manufacture of consumer goods. They experimented with new approaches; collective farms were joined into larger units, virgin lands were opened in Siberia, peasants were paid higher prices for their produce, and Western methods and machines were tried in Soviet agriculture and industry. The growth rate of the Soviet economy remained impressive. More than half of the Soviet Union's industry was built in the period after World War II. So high, indeed, was the growth rate of the Soviet economy in the late 1950's that Khrushchev boasted that the U.S.S.R. would catch up with the U.S.A. by 1970.

The rapid growth of Soviet industry was due partly to centralized state planning, which permitted the concentration of effort in particular industries and the total mobilization of manpower. Exercising political and economic control over the people, the government could assign workers to specific jobs. It prodded them on to maximum exertion by publicly honoring "heroes of Socialist labor" and by paying workers according to the amount they produced. The speed of Soviet industrialization was facilitated by the fact that the U.S.S.R. had gotten a late start, in that the Russians could apply the inventions and techniques developed elsewhere. Many foreign engineers and technicians were employed in the Soviet Union in the 1930's.

The actual rate of growth of the Soviet economy has been a matter of controversy. Soviet writers come up with impressive figures by dating Russian industrialization from the late 1920's. Western economists counter that Soviet industrialization did not begin from scratch. The industrialization of Russia started in the late nineteenth century; in spite of the destruction of the civil war, the Soviets inherited the basic resources and skills necessary for industrialization. Nor has the Soviet Union been able to maintain its predicted rate of growth. There has been a definite slackening of pace since 1958. With the attainment of a heavy-industry base, Soviet growth has become increasingly dependent on consumer production, yet the Soviet system is insufficiently responsive to consumer demands.

In the Soviet Union most goods and services are supplied by state enterprises. A small percentage are furnished by cooperatives and a very tiny percentage by private enterprises. The state enterprises are founded, financed, and operated by the state. Profits and losses are also taken by the state. Factory directors and their senior staff members receive financial bonuses, as well as other incentives such as better housing and vacations, for fulfilling and particularly for over-fulfilling the quotas set by the government. To succeed in their production goals, directors often find it necessary to make deals with other directors to insure for their factory the necessary raw materials and supplies; sometimes they set up their own workshops to manufacture needed parts. The most detailed

planning cannot provide for everything without error, and these and other informal arrangements are necessary to make the Soviet economy work.

State enterprises include industrial factories, construction works, state farms, trade and material supply organizations, and foreign trade corporations. Cooperative enterprises include producers' cooperatives, which make such goods as musical instruments, furniture, and clothes. Operating funds are obtained from government banks, and the enterprises may be expanded from profits. Profits are taxed at a rising rate—a tax of about 20 percent is levied on profits

The pictures of Leningrad workers, honored as "heroes of Socialist labor," call on the public to follow their example.

below 5 percent of production costs; a tax of 90 percent is levied on profits above 15 percent of production costs.

A limited amount of private enterprise exists in the Soviet Union. A person may make things for sale, but he may not employ another person to help him do so. He may, furthermore, sell what he himself has produced; he may not sell what someone else has produced. For example, it is legal for a shoemaker to set up a little booth and make or repair shoes; it is illegal for him to hire another shoemaker as his assistant. It is legal for a farmer to sell melons he has grown; it is illegal for someone else to buy the melons and resell them.

The extent of Soviet industrial progress is uneven. Guided by the desire to strengthen the U.S.S.R. quickly, Soviet planners assigned certain priorities. The series of five-year plans provided for leaps forward in particular areas, with resources and publicity concentrated in those areas. The rest of the economy was left to fall behind until a new campaign led to a leap forward in *that* area of industry. Such "leapfrogging" was wasteful in that each separate effort was overdone and efficiency was lost in areas that were permitted to fall behind. On the other hand, greater enthusiasm for catching up in areas in which the country was lagging could be generated.

The increase in steel production was particularly remarkable, boosting the U.S.S.R. to second place in the world. In ore production, too, the Soviet Union became second only to the United States. It became first in output of coal and iron ore, metal-cutting lathes, and electric and diesel locomotives. Communist methods alone could not have achieved this progress, however. The Soviet Union's industrial growth depended largely on the enormous natural resources of the land. These included about 60 percent of the world's coal deposits, nearly half of its oil, over 40 percent of its iron ore, almost 90 percent of its manganese, one-quarter of its timber land, over a half of its potassium salts, and nearly one-third of its phosphates.

In an economy that was not based on the demands of the market, the laws of supply and demand, which operate in a private enterprise system, did not regulate production. While local officials were in a

A street sweeper and a shoe cleaner in conversation. Women form a large part of the Soviet labor force.

position to know local needs best and while decentralization of industry and agriculture was tried from time to time with success, local officials did not see the whole picture. Planning for the country as a whole had to be done centrally in Moscow. On the other hand, the problems of planning in an industrial economy became so complicated as to overwhelm the leaders. While campaigns helped to arouse the workers' enthusiasm and gave them standards or goals of production against which to judge their work, many plans had been conceived too hastily to be effective. Furthermore, as noted already, the income of the workers was kept down as the government used some of the profits to pay for state enterprises. When workers and peasants failed to respond to governmental exhortations, strong measures were taken to force them to comply.

The Communist leaders were not swayed by hardships. In their view, extreme industrial and agricultural efforts were necessary in the war that the Soviet Union was waging with the capitalist world. If one looks at the Soviet economy as a "war economy," its measures resemble in some respects those taken by the Western countries during World War II, when governments allocated resources to certain projects and not to others and strove for technological breakthroughs in particular areas, such as the development of radar and the atom bomb.

In the 1920's economic measures in the U.S.S.R. were overshadowed by political considerations. In their determination to wipe out free enterprise and private farming, Communist planners were not primarily concerned with cost and growth. Now that most of the economy has been nationalized, political considerations are less important. Today the state seeks economically sound solutions to the many problems that state enterprise poses.

The rules of employment are changing. While graduates of institutions of higher learning and technical schools are assigned to particular jobs for a number of years and while members of the Communist party and of the Communist Youth Organization may be sent anywhere, most workers are now free to quit their jobs without penalty, if they find other employment within a month. Soviet trade unions can negotiate for improved working conditions, but not for better wages. Their primary function is to assist in carrying out party economic policies. Thus, it is the freedom of workers to choose employment that has driven wages upward, as managers seek to attract and hold better workers.

Prices of goods in the Soviet Union are set by the government. They may or may not be related to the cost of production. Prices are used by the government for political purposes as well as for economic purposes. For example, books with a propaganda message are more attractively priced than scholarly volumes, and the phonograph disk of cosmonaut Yury Gagarin's voice from outer space costs a fraction of the price of a popular recording. At the same time by keeping the price of necessities such as shoes, shirts, and suits, which everyone must buy, fairly high (at two or three times their cost in the United States) the government, which owns the factories, can also make sufficient profit to pay for less popular projects and to keep direct taxes low.

Soviet agriculture continues to lag. Almost half the people still work the land, yet they are unable to obtain the sort of food surplus that would free them for industrial work and permit large-scale export. In fact, in the 1960's the Soviet Union has had to import millions of tons of wheat from the United States, Canada, and Australia. The reasons for Soviet problems in agriculture are in part climatic and geographical. But they are also ideological. Marxist preoccupation with industrialization led to the neglect of agriculture.

Agriculture, like industry, is controlled by the state. The collective farms are a form of cooperative enterprise. They are cooperatives of peasants of a given area who live on nationalized land without paying rent. The peasants participate in determining work rules and distribution of income; they elect a committee and a chairman to manage the farm. But the election of the chairman is really controlled by the party secretary of the region, and production quotas are set by the state. Until 1958, the state controlled the activities of the collective farms also by concentrating all power-driven machinery in the hands of state Machinery Tractor Stations (which have since been disbanded, machines now being owned by the farms themselves).

The collective farms must deliver a certain quota of produce to the state or to consumer-cooperatives. In addition, individual members as well as the collective farm as a whole may sell excess produce at a somewhat higher price on the free or collective farm markets maintained by towns. The collective farm workers do not receive a definite salary; they are not guaranteed a minimum wage. Their pay, partly in money, partly in farm products, depends on the amount of produce available (after expenses and obligations of the farm have been met) and on the num-

This well-appointed department store reflects the increasing availability of consumer goods in the Soviet economy.

ber of days worked. As peasants generally cannot live on the resultant wage, they are allowed to own some livestock and to cultivate a small plot of land. While the right of the peasant to sell excess produce on the market forms a very important source of income for his family, it represents a waste of millions of man-days because of the time taken by the peasants to travel back and forth to sell a few things themselves.

On state farms pay is better because the salary of the farm workers is regarded as a fixed expenditure that must be met. Until recently at least, collective farms were responsible for their own social security, while state farmers were treated as factory workers with pensions and other forms of state assistance. Like the collective farmers, state farm workers and other rural inhabitants usually are allowed to own some livestock and cultivate small plots of land. Even urban workers supplement their diet with what they can raise in vegetable gardens.

It is difficult to evaluate the present state of the Soviet economy because it is so unevenly developed. The contrast between urban and rural Russia in terms of modernization is startling. Few modern highways bind the country together. In spite of her enormous size, the Soviet Union had in 1960, in terms of miles, only about one-fourth as many roads as the United States. Her railroads numbered only about one-third of those in the United States in mileage. But in aviation she outdistanced the United States; and as air transportation is making great strides, she may develop her transportation system in leapfrog fashion more rapidly than statistics suggest. Similarly, while in some areas several people are permitted to do a job that really could be handled by one person, great advances in automation are being made in heavy industry.

In the economic race, to which the Soviet Union has challenged the United States, she has certain advantages. Her system allows her to maintain a high rate of investment regardless of individual preferences or business fluctuations. Her continued concentration on heavy industry and basic products such as minerals, steel, and fuel results in economic growth. Because it can guarantee continued production of a particular model or type, her system is suited for long-range planning and automation. The channeling of a large percentage of her best students into science is likely to increase the rate of scientific achievements.

The Soviet economic system also has definite handicaps in the race with the United States. It fails to provide adequate incentives for managers and workers to do their utmost. Soviet planning and methods of farm production remain inefficient. The U.S.S.R. has great difficulty in relating production and supply decisions and in adjusting production to demands. Her resources are repeatedly misdirected. Above all, the needs of an economy that is still developing and of one that is already developed differ, and the required switch in policy as the Soviet economy changes from a developing one to a developed one has begun to slow the growth rate. The system that the Soviet Union has found successful in building an industrial state may not be equally successful in running it, once it has been built.

Since the end of 1965 the Soviet economy has been experimenting with some basic changes on a national scale, comparable in importance to the introduction of the New Economic Plan in 1921 and the

In the Soviet Union demand still exceeds supply. There are lines for everything, including taxicabs.

series of five-year plans in 1928. Instead of the "command system" of production, involving centralized planning in minute detail, central planners are to work through industrial ministries. As one seasoned observer explains it:

> Under the ministries, the managers of individual enterprises, absolute bosses, are to be given broad targets and then left free to produce the best they can. Their finance is to be so arranged that they will sink or swim by the profits or losses they make.
>
> Of course, the profits will not go to individual shareholders. The state is the only shareholder and will receive interest on longterm credits for capital equipment as well as a share of the profits. The rest of the profits will be at the disposal of the management to be used for plowing back and for incentive payments in the form of higher wages and special bonuses.[5]

This does not mean that the Soviet Union is on the road to capitalism. It does mean that the U.S.S.R. realizes that a certain relaxation of controls is necessary in the economic field, as in other areas, to stimulate progress.

FIVE

GOVERNMENT

Autocracy is deeply rooted in Russian history. It goes back to Byzantine and Mongol times. Russia was not without some democratic traditions—councils of princes and popular assemblies—but these faded as the country, preoccupied with defense and national consolidation, seemed to need a strong government. In this respect Russia does not differ from other lands where powerful kings overcame feudal states and self-governing cities. Rather, it was the failure of Russia to shed its absolute form of government once it had outlived historical usefulness and justification that separates it from other countries.

What impressed Peter the Great about the West was not parliamentary government but administrative efficiency. Though the names of some of the political institutions that subsequently came into existence sounded as if there were representative government in eighteenth- and nineteenth-century Russia—"Governing Senate" and "Council of State," for example—their members were appointed or nominated by the Tsar, in whose hands authority firmly remained. In the second half of the nineteenth century local government was reorganized, with elected land assemblies and urban municipal councils receiving a certain amount of self-government. The land assemblies, for example, built schools, hospitals, and orphanages; they organized experimental farms, imported agricultural machinery, and established banks where peasants could borrow money on reasonable terms. Yet the resources and privileges of the local institutions were extremely limited.

At the beginning of the twentieth century, the Tsar still held "supreme autocratic and unlimited power." This does not mean, of course, that he ruled singlehandedly or made all key decisions himself. He appointed a State Council to advise him and gave its members considerable powers. Eleven ministries and an elaborate bureaucracy formed the national administration. After the Revolution of 1905, the State Council was transformed into the upper house of a parliament, with the newly created Duma as the lower house.

The Duma had limited powers and the ministers were not responsible to it. It was dissolved three times and hindered at every turn. Yet its very existence was an important step toward constitutional government. Legislative control of the two chambers limited the autocratic powers of the Tsar, and the people participated through elected representatives in the conduct of public affairs. To be sure, the right to vote was still limited, and most representatives belonged to the land-owning class. But it was a start in the political education of the people, and it is possible that in time democratic institutions might have evolved in Russia as in other countries.

School children waiting to see Lenin's body. The banner of Lenin, Engels, and Marx is inscribed "To the victory of Communism!"

With the overthrow of the monarchy in March of 1917, democracy seemed within reach. A Provisional Government was established by the Duma to run the country until representatives could be assembled to write a constitution. Although the Provisional Government was not permitted to do anything that would predetermine the eventual form of government that the assembly was to fashion, its democratic sentiments were clear. But the Provisional Government's determination not to desert the Allies in World War I contributed to its downfall.

The Communist Revolution reversed the trend toward democracy and imposed a totalitarian dictatorship more absolute in power and control than the autocracy of old. Though Marx and Lenin spoke of democracy to gain followers, Russian Marxists did not believe that the people were ready for self-government. The Marxists felt that although peasants and workers demanded the right of self-government in order to obtain better living conditions, they would not know how to act effectively. Lenin and his followers insisted on the need for leadership by a small dedicated group that knew how to build a Communist state.

Marxism-Leninism envisaged two stages in the transformation from capitalism to communism: (1) from capitalism (where the means of production were in the hands of private individuals) to socialism (where the means of production were owned by the state) and (2) from socialism to communism (where the means of production belonged to everyone). During the first period, the country must be guided by a dictatorship of the proletariat (the absolute rule of the Communist leaders on behalf of the working class). During the second period, when the economic needs of the people had been met and the masses were educated to abide by the rules of socialist life, the strong hand of dictatorship would no longer be needed. The state itself (as Engels put it) would "wither away." Officially, the Soviet Union has completed the first phase and now claims to be on the road toward communism. But in spite of the relative relaxation in political, economic, social, and cultural control following the death of Stalin, the state shows no signs of withering away.

The Union of Soviet Socialist Republics is a federation of fifteen Soviet Socialist Republics, each with a government patterned after the central government. The federation is not as loose or as decentralized as in the United States or Canada, however, and while the various republics theoretically are self-governing, they are in fact subject to the central government.

According to the Constitution of 1936 the country is governed by the Supreme Soviet (or Supreme Council), which is a parliament consisting of two houses: the Council of the Union, elected on the basis of population, and the Council of Nationalities, elected on the basis of national regions and territory. Both houses are equal in power, bills having to pass both to become law. The Supreme Soviet chooses a body of officials, known as the Presidium (formerly called the Central Executive Committee), and a President as ceremonial head of state. It also appoints the Council of Ministers (formerly known as the Council of People's Commissars) as chief executive agency. There is little separation of legislative, executive, and judicial powers.

The Supreme Soviet is elected by universal suffrage. Every citizen over eighteen years of age (except "the insane and persons sentenced by a court to deprivation of their electoral rights") is entitled to vote by secret ballot. But a citizen's choice of candidates is limited to those nominated by the Communist party and by such nonpolitical public organizations as trade unions, which are also dominated by the party. Voters may cross out the names of candidates but may not write in others. Furthermore, they are not required to fold their ballots secretly in a booth, but can do so publicly in the open room. As many do not use the booth, the more timid citizens are inclined not to do so either, lest their action be interpreted as a vote against the official list of candidates and thus against the regime.

The Supreme Soviet and lower Soviets are limited in real power. The Supreme Soviet meets once or twice a year for only a few days. Even then its sessions are taken up primarily by long speeches by the leaders. The Presidium has authority to act in place of the Supreme Soviet when it is not in session. During its brief meetings the Supreme Soviet gives general approval of the budget, confirms the decrees issued by the Presidium, and votes unanimously for the decisions made in advance of the session by the Presidium.

The Communist party is the Soviet Union's leadership group. It is the one and only political party allowed in the U.S.S.R. While it raises funds, nominates candidates, and works for their election, it is not really a political party in the Western sense. Not every Soviet citizen can join it; and if he does, his role within the party is quite different from that of the average registered Democrat or Republican in the

United States. Though the Soviet voter is given the impression that he chooses his leaders and influences policy, there are no direct elections for top Communist officials and the representatives he selects to the Supreme Soviet and local Soviets have little political power. Not only do voters at large merely approve or disapprove the list of candidates put on the ballot by the Communist party but rank-and-file party members also have no part in composing the list. Nominations are made by a small number of highly placed Communist officials.

The Communist party has the centralized organization, chain of command, and discipline of an army, rather than that of a political party. Membership is limited to a small portion of the population—less than 10 percent of the Soviet people are "card-carrying Communists." Would-be members are carefully screened and tested for their political reliability, zeal, and willingness to take orders. At party meetings they have the right to stand up and be heard. However, they are not allowed to meet together with other members in advance of their speech for the purposes of seeking support or winning votes for their respective projects. In other words, individual party members are not in a position to oppose policy from above effectively.

The Communist party structure parallels that of the government. Side by side with the Supreme Soviet there is an All-Union Congress of the party. The All-Union Congress elects a Central Committee, and the latter in turn elects a Presidium (formerly called the Politburo).

In theory the Communist party and the government are separate; in fact, however, the Communist party dominates the government. Top party leaders hold key positions in the government. Thus Stalin was both Chairman of the Council of Ministers and First Secretary of the Communist party. Through the men he appointed to the Presidium of the party and to other strategic positions in party and government he ruled arbitrarily, eliminating actual and imagined opposition by terror and force. The system Lenin had created provided no safeguards against the seizure of power by one man. Stalin, operating from the strategic position of secretary of the party, took advantage of it and established a personal dictatorship.

In the years between 1936 and 1939 many important Communists—top party leaders, journalists, and high ranking army officers—were accused of treason, forced to "confess" at public trials, and executed. Meanwhile, tens of thousands of ordinary members were expelled from the party, and the common people were terrorized by mass arrests. Although no one was safe from imprisonment and condemnation without trial to forced labor camps or exile in Siberia and other remote parts of the Soviet Union, former members of opposition groups within the Communist party, former members of other parties, members of national minorities, and persons with relatives and friends abroad were favorite targets.

The elimination or suspension of terror as a policy of state and the less active role of the secret police following the death of Stalin have loosened, but not ended, the government's control of the people. Communist party members, who are in every walk of life, remain the eyes, ears, and mouths of the state. They report potential opponents to the Communist authorities. They help spread among the people the "party

On political holidays the U.S.S.R. becomes a sea of slogans. "Peace, labor, freedom, equality, brotherhood, happiness" sits atop "Glory to the Party of Lenin!"

line," fed them by special pamphlets for agitators, by special instructions, and by *Pravda*, the official newspaper of the party. They assist in carrying out party policy by voting at nonpolitical meetings of various sorts in accordance with the desires of the party.

The influence of the Communist party radiates to the young people and their families through Communist youth organizations: the Young Octobrists (political Cub Scouts and Brownies of a sort), the Pioneers (political Boy Scouts and Girl Scouts), and the Komsomols (Communist Youth Leaguers between the ages of fourteen and twenty-six). Though there are many admirable features to the Pioneer movement—the children receive excellent free instruction in art, music, foreign languages, baking, and the like—it results in political indoctrination of the children as well. The older Komsomols are sent to labor on such projects as building a subway or tilling virgin land in order to encourage adult citizens to volunteer for similar work; they also assist teachers and professors in maintaining discipline. In a university dormitory, for example, standards of conduct are set and enforced by a Komsomol Committee. The Communist party, therefore, uses the Komsomol not only to train potential party members but to influence and control the lives of all young people and their elders.

The Soviet army and the courts of law also are dominated by the Communist party. The army is, of course, a major pillar of support. Many officers and men are members of the Communist party, and political commissars (officials) are attached to units to indoctrinate the troops and keep a check on the commanders. At the same time the loyalty of the army is encouraged by special privileges, ranks, titles, and fine uniforms. The courts of law are another instrument of government policy. They do not uphold the rights of the citizens from encroachment by the state; they are not impartial; they do not act as checks and balances on the executive and legislative branches of the government. More than half of the lower-level judges and most, if not all, higher-level judges are members of the Communist party.

While the leaders in the Kremlin shape and enforce policy through the Communist party and through party-dominated organizations, they continue to claim that their government is democratic. The Constitution of 1936, drafted under Stalin, at first reading appears to guarantee the basic freedoms of a democratic society. Article 125 states:

> In conformity with the interests of the working people, and in order to strengthen the socialist system, the citizens of the U.S.S.R. are guaranteed by law:
> (a) freedom of speech;
> (b) freedom of the press;
> (c) freedom of assembly, including the holding of mass meetings;
> (d) freedom of street processions and demonstrations.
>
> These civil rights are ensured by placing at the disposal of the working people and their organizations printing presses, stocks of paper, public buildings, the streets, communications facilities and other material requisites for the exercise of these rights.[6]

On second reading, the qualifications "in conformity with the interests of the working people" and "in order to strengthen the socialist system" stand out as crucial limitations. Nor does the placing of printing presses, paper, and the like into the hands of "the working people and their organizations" guarantee free speech. On the contrary, it leaves opposing views unprinted. As Stalin himself remarked approvingly: "I must admit that the draft of the new constitution actually leaves in force the regime of the dictatorship of the working class as well as preserves unchanged the present leading position of the Communist party." Khrushchev, before his ouster, called for the drafting of a new constitution designed to "prepare conditions for the transition to communist and public self-government." It is unlikely that a new constitution will deprive the Communist party of its monopoly of power; on the contrary, the role of the Communist party is likely to increase.

The fact that rights that are given with one hand are taken away with the other is typical of the Soviet system. It has democratic forms that are counterweighted with totalitarian controls and thus are not allowed to function freely. The government manipulates people by giving them the *illusion* of democracy; it tries to keep them satisfied by making them believe that they participate in government. And, in a sense, they participate all the time. Not only do Soviet citizens vote, as mentioned already, but they are asked to sign countless petitions—now for nuclear disarmament, now against American "imperialism"—to demonstrate "spontaneously," to take part in production drives, and to attend meeting after meeting. Thus they are made to feel that their signatures and presence are important, that the government depends on their participation and support.

The tradition of Russian intellectuals and revolutionaries who criticized the government at great sacri-

The government uses newspapers, such as the Communist party's Pravda, *to mold public opinion.*

fice to themselves is not dead. The number of Soviet citizens "liquidated" or sent to labor camps is a constant reminder of opposition. Great was the courage of Soviet authors who smuggled their manuscripts out for publication abroad. The average person, of course, does not want to be a hero. Nor is he as concerned with freedom of expression. When he runs into various restrictions, he does not oppose them. He accepts them or finds ways of getting around them.

The Soviet citizen cannot move about freely. He cannot hop on a train and go wherever he pleases without permission. He carries a domestic passport and must receive permission to stay in one place or another. He rarely can go abroad; and even when he enters a library, institute, or dormitory in his own country, he must present his credentials. He is kept ever mindful of the danger of associating with foreigners, who are depicted as would-be spies.

But the Soviet Union is not now a police state in the sense that policemen are all-present. The secret police, still dreaded, are in the background. The militiamen who direct traffic and patrol the streets are accommodating and gentle, and take far more abuse from the citizens than most American policemen would. Volunteer policemen are more enthusiastic and less professional in their maintenance of order, but even they do not dominate the scene. After almost half a century of education and indoctrination, the Communists have conditioned the people to their environment. State ownership of the means of production and government leadership are generally accepted principles.

The forceful oppression of the Stalin days is past and, hopefully, will not return. "With Stalin we made a great mistake, which must not and will not be repeated," a Soviet student writes confidently. It is likely that a certain relaxation of controls will continue because of changes in Soviet society. Managers and technicians have attained important positions and influence outside the party, while within the party educated people, who once formed a minority, have become the majority and have sought a greater share in decision making. Yet so long as communism remains the goal—and there is no reason to believe that it will not—democratization will be limited, for as Marx and Lenin realized, if the people were given unrestricted freedom of expression and political action, they might well choose a different path.

SIX

EDUCATION

Soviet space flights and missile exploits have focused attention on education in the U.S.S.R. At the public school level, Russian students receive intensive instruction in the natural sciences as well as in the humanities. In part this is due to a systematic and fixed program which emphasizes solid courses and facts in the Soviet Union; in part this is due to an intellectual tradition which goes back to Tsarist times.

Different schools, run by churches, brotherhoods of monks, and private masters, appeared in the sixteenth century. Peter the Great established a School of Mathematical and Navigation Sciences at Moscow and laid the foundations for the Academy of Sciences, which was opened in 1725. Other public and private institutions were founded in the eighteenth century, including the state universities of St. Petersburg and Moscow. During the reign of Catherine the Great, a few free primary and secondary schools open not only to the nobility but to all classes were introduced by the state. Following the Great Reforms of Alexander II in the nineteenth century, primary education was

Students of Public School 238 in Leningrad. They are majoring in English and after two years of study speak it remarkably well.

furthered by the provincial and district land assemblies. Attempts by the Duma after 1905 to establish compulsory primary education were blocked by church school supporters, but the public school system was considerably expanded before the Revolution of 1917. This is not to say that education was general; sixty percent or more of the population was illiterate. But the foundations for universal education had been laid.

The educational system in Tsarist times was European in character. Pupils came from all classes of society, but it was an "elite" system in that it catered to the brighter students rather than to everyone. Instruction was difficult, and much homework was required. The system was authoritarian in the sense that the teachers exercised great authority and the students took prescribed courses, rather than what they pleased. There was strict discipline and a "no nonsense" approach, with few athletic or social activities.

Tsarist restrictions on free speech and political activity are well known. Yet it should be pointed out that the Russian universities, like their European counterparts, had considerable self-government by the second half of the nineteenth century, electing their own administration and professors. Faculty members were very outspoken and students were in the forefront of revolutionary agitation.

In the decade following the Communist Revolution, education (like literature, art, and practically every other field of endeavor) was an area of experimentation. "Progressive education" attracted much attention. Practical vocational training was combined with subject-matter study. But the students graduated semiliterate. The five-year plans demanded specialists, and the traditional methods of instruction were revived to supply them. Similarly the authority of the teacher, which had been undermined following the Revolution, was revived, for attractive as equality of student and teacher may have been in theory, it disrupted instruction.

In the 1920's and early 1930's, Communist party schools were organized to train leaders in the most important professions. The party schools, like other innovations, were gradually abandoned. Desperately in need of educated men to plan and run its economy and state, the Soviet government went back to a modified form of the old educational system. As the latter had been patterned to a large extent on European models, Soviet education, except for its Communist slant, was also basically European in character.

The Soviet system differed from the old system most strikingly in its attempt to reach the masses at the same time that it trained an elite and in its desire to indoctrinate the students for life in a Communist state. Students were regarded as resources which, like other national resources, needed development for the good of the country.

Education in the Soviet Union begins with the kindergartens, which are provided by the state, factories, or collective farms. The kindergartens, for children from three to seven years of age, prepare the youngsters for entrance to elementary school by giving them some knowledge of words and figures and by teaching them habits of work and cooperation as well as love of country and government. The emphasis in preschool education, as in later informal schooling, is on purposeful training for life—in terms of development of technical skills, social adjustment, and patri-

otism—rather than on development of the individual personality. The program is carefully planned on a national basis.

A child begins primary school, which lasts for four years, at the age of seven. Students go to school six days a week and receive much homework. They learn to read, write, and calculate and obtain some introductory knowledge of science. They all take the same courses and usually have the same teacher for the four years.

Until the end of 1958 secondary school generally was divided into "incomplete secondary school" and

In the Palace of Pioneers in Moscow young students get supplementary instruction in such fields as music, painting, cooking, and communism.

"complete secondary school." Incomplete secondary school was for persons planning to become skilled workers and semiprofessionals. At about the age of fourteen, students went directly from the incomplete secondary school to vocational and technical schools (lasting two to four years) or to factory training schools (lasting six months to a year). At these institutions students learned, for example, about railroad work and mining. Pupils continued their studies at the complete secondary school until the age of seventeen. From there they could enter various technical schools to become highly skilled workers and junior technical personnel (after another year to a year and a half of training) or universities, learned academies, and institutes for professional training (this required four to six years of study).

From primary school on, courses were difficult and required much homework. They were specialized, with various teachers handling different subjects. Heavy emphasis was placed on science; over 40 percent of the offerings dealt with science and mathematics, including some six years of biology, five years of physics, and four years of chemistry. As in primary school, all students studied the same subject matter, selected and planned in such a way as to provide the state with technically skilled and politically loyal citizens.

But the students were so absorbed in their studies, it seemed to Khrushchev and the party, that they lost touch with the toil and sweat of life and did not develop a love for physical labor. In 1958, therefore, the school system was revised. Compulsory education was extended from seven to eight years. The secondary school now was to train people who, in addition to knowing the foundations of learning, were capable of systematic physical labor, were educated to serve society, and could actively participate in production. In line with Khrushchev's desire to bridge the gap between workers and intellectuals, students were to be employed for two years before entering the university. But the labor in which secondary and would-be university students engaged reluctantly was neither productive nor conducive to love of work. At the same time it took away too much time from their studies. As a result, in 1964, two months before Khrushchev's fall from power, a reorganization of the school system was begun. It has not yet been completed.

In many respects the Soviet school system has been successful. According to Soviet statistics, illiteracy of those over ten years old was reduced from 49 percent in 1926 to 19 percent in 1939. The current illiteracy rate is between 5 percent and 10 percent. Education is mostly tuition-free, and the cost of living in a university dormitory is nominal. Eight out of ten Soviet students receive a modest living allowance for studying at the university. Not only can students of ability, if they seem politically reliable, have their way paid through school, but they are assured of a position upon graduation.

On the other hand, the state determines in what fields scholarships will be available, and students are channeled into areas in which they may not be interested. Furthermore, recipients of scholarships usually are required to work for several years in a given position. Thus the strength of the Soviet system from a national point of view is to provide the economy with skills that are needed. The Soviet Union, for example, is graduating about twice as many engineers and agricultural experts as the United States. The weakness of the system, from the individual point of view, is that the desires of the individual may not be heeded. Only a small percentage of students are able to pursue the humanities and liberal arts.

Science has flourished partly because there is relatively little politics involved in scientific research. A scientist is relatively free to make full use of his abilities without endangering his position. A historian, on the other hand, must stay within the bounds of Marxism-Leninism and must adjust himself to shifts in

party line. He has neither the financial rewards nor the security of a natural scientist. The weakness in science education has been in narrow specialization; some scientists excel in a very limited area without comprehending the field as a whole.

The Soviets have also made great progress in the teaching of foreign languages. There are a number of English, German, French, and other secondary schools in which the children, in addition to the regular general education curriculum, receive concentrated language instruction. The results are impressive; students about nine or ten years old are able to converse quite

Photographs of the best Pioneers are displayed in front of the Palace of Pioneers in Leningrad. Public praise and blame are common Soviet ways of guiding the actions and conduct of the people.

freely in a foreign language. Furthermore, the Russians have considerable experience in teaching Russian to people with another native tongue. While schools in the various republics are conducted in the language of the region, all students are also taught Russian.

Political propaganda proceeds along with learning. For example, in their English class, the students sing songs about the Young Communist League; when discussing English literature, they are taught what Lenin liked about the writings of Jack London, who criticized capitalist society.

Communist influence is felt throughout the school system through party directives and the work of Communist Youth Leaguers. Many of the values that are taught in Soviet schools and youth organizations are universal: to obey parents and teachers, to study diligently, to tell the truth, to help fellow students, to respect property, to be polite, to be punctual, and not to make too much noise. They are supplemented, however, by a strong dose of patriotism and loyalty to communism. Children are taught not only to love their motherland but to love Lenin and to be grateful to the Communist party and the Soviet government.

Discipline on the primary and secondary school level is strict, and an American visitor will be impressed to see students rise when the teacher enters the class or when they answer a question. On the university level, on the other hand, students conduct themselves much like Americans. They have greater motivation because education is a more important factor in economic and social success than in the United States, but they find life as distracting as their American counterparts. Great sportsmen and lovers of the ballet, the opera, and classical music, and just as intent on having a good time as college students elsewhere, Russians cut classes, cram before exams, and try to outguess their teachers.

The greatest problem Soviet students and their professors face is their relative isolation from foreign ideas and reliable sources. They cannot travel abroad as freely as did intellectuals before the Revolution; they do not have access, as a rule, to non-Communist newspapers; and the card catalogues in libraries are highly selective and only partially open to the public. Soviet histories and reference books change with the party line. Individuals are purged not only from the government but from history. Thus Stalin was removed from the mausoleum and painted out of a well-known picture that he had shared with Lenin; Lenin now is reading his thoughts to an empty chair.

But in education, as in art and literature, there has been some relaxation since the death of Stalin. The exposure of some of Stalin's crimes made a deep impression on Soviet university students. They were shocked not only by the cruel deeds that had been committed in the name of communism but by the revelation that many of the facts that they had been taught had been lies. Henceforth they are bound to be more skeptical about what they read, and some recent publications in history and economics have shown a greater degree of objectivity than in the past.

SEVEN

RELIGION

The Russian Orthodox Church is a part of the Orthodox Eastern Church, a community of independent Christian churches which officially split from the Roman Catholic or Western Church in the eleventh century. The highest bishop, the patriarch, of Constantinople dominated its affairs until the sixteenth century, when it became independent of the Greek Church. It was not equally independent from its own state, however. Not only did the clergy heed the wishes of the Tsar but the Tsar used the church to strengthen his rule with religious authority. In the eighteenth century Peter the Great formally established state control over the church. From early times, therefore, the Russian Orthodox Church was not the master or rival, but the servant, of the government. The same was true of the various religious minorities that were incorporated into the Russian domain as the empire expanded.

Like the Roman Catholic Church, the Eastern Orthodox Church bases its creed and dogma on the Old and New Testaments, the writings of the church fathers, and the decisions of the ecumenical councils. Like the Roman Catholic Church, it celebrates seven sacraments, but it has somewhat different views about the meaning and the administration of the sacraments. In addition, some of the doctrines differ from those of the Roman Catholic Church. For example, the Eastern Orthodox Church believes that the Holy Ghost proceeds directly from God, rather than from God and from Christ; it venerates the Virgin Mary but does not accept her Immaculate Conception. Unlike the Roman Catholic Church, it allows the congregation to partake of the bread and wine during the celebration of the Lord's Supper, holy communion being given with a long spoon.

The worshippers stand throughout the long service, falling onto their knees and touching their foreheads to the floor occasionally. The entire service, in old Slavonic, is always sung, without the aid of any musical instruments. Unlike their Roman Catholic brethren, Russian Orthodox parish priests traditionally can marry; indeed they must marry before being ordained. They can marry only once, however. Widowers become eligible for monkhood and promotion, bishops being traditionally chosen from among the monks. The Russian Orthodox Church, like the Orthodox Eastern Church in general, believes in the equality of the patriarchs and refuses to recognize the supreme authority of the Pope.

For the average Russian before the Revolution—uneducated and illiterate—the beauty and majesty of the church service, with its sung litany, its choral music, its candles, incense, and costly robes, was an emotional rather than an intellectual experience. His knowledge of the scriptures was scanty. Indeed, often the parish priests knew little more about church doctrines than did the worshippers. This did not diminish the religious devotion of the faithful who sought a mystical direct communion with God. They observed long and strict fasts, crowded into countless churches, with their ever-ringing bells, and stood through lengthy night services.

The role of the church in Russia, as in the West, was not confined to religion, for religion until modern times was not divorced from daily life. The Russian Church for centuries inspired art, music, literature, and education. Its influence was less constraining than is often thought, however, since it allowed complete intellectual freedom, providing a certain nominal allegiance to the church was shown. So long as a person did not desert or openly attack the church, he could advance scientific theories inconsistent with religious doctrine. Yet in the event of public opposition, the church insisted on complete acceptance of its dogma.

The church was controlled by the state. Though the Tsar did not become head of the church in name (as did Protestant rulers), he dominated it by appointing key church officials and a civilian chief procurator, who had authority over them. The close relationship between church and state was of mutual advantage. As the official custodian of the state religion, the church received exclusive state support and could call on the government to punish anyone who deserted the church or its beliefs. In return, the church preached that it was the religious duty of all subjects to submit to the will of the Tsar. The Orthodox Church, as an agency of Tsarism, was partner also to the attempt to Russianize the minorities of the empire. But the close relationship between state and

The star-topped May pole on Moscow's Red Square overshadows the crosses of the Cathedral of St. Basil the Blessed.

church proved fatal. The political support which the Russian Orthodox Church gave to the autocracy eventually condemned it, along with the monarchy, in the eyes of reformers and revolutionaries.

Many intellectuals opposed the Russian Orthodox Church on religious and philosophical grounds, contending that it stood in the way of God. The famous novelist Leo Tolstoy turned his back on the church. An ardent advocate of what one might call "applied Christianity," he was a social reformer and pacifist. He treasured the teachings of Jesus, but not the dogmas and rites of organized religion. The poet-philosopher Vladimir Solovyev expounded a deeply mystical view of Christianity; and the author Dimitry Merezhkovskii and his wife, a poet and a critic herself, worked through the Religious and Philosophical Society to instill religious feeling in the intelligentsia. In short, it was characteristic of Russian writers to seek salvation and, as one of them expressed it, to "suffer for the world."

Other intellectuals turned away from mysticism and pious feeling, as well as from the church. Russia's salvation, they argued, lay in civilization, enlightenment, and humanity. As the celebrated literary critic Vissarion Belinsky wrote:

> What she needs is not sermons (she has heard enough of them!) or prayers (she has repeated them too often!), but the awakening in the people of a sense of human dignity lost for so many centuries amid the dirt and refuse; she needs rights and laws conforming not with the preaching of the church but with common sense and justice, and their strictest possible observance. Instead of which she presents the dire spectacle of a country where men traffic in men, without even having the excuse so insidiously ex-

Most Russian churches, like the cathedral in Leningrad, are now hollow shells—architectural museum pieces.

ploited by the American plantation owners who claim that the Negro is not a man. . . .[7]

The intelligentsia's dislike of the established church smoothed the path for the full-scale attack against the church following the overthrow of the monarchy. The failure of the Russian Orthodox Church to take an interest in social problems—to remain a "living" church—eased the task of the Communists.

Karl Marx had called religion the opiate of the people—a drug that dulled their pain. He believed that it was used by the ruling classes to keep the people submissive. The abolition of the church thus became a major goal of Communist revolutionaries. When they came to power they seized the property of the church. The church buildings, once they had been taken over by the government, could be leased from the state by communities of believers. But most churches were closed. Some were destroyed; others converted into theaters, skating rinks, and apartment houses. A number of the most beautiful ones became architectural museums. Religious philosophers were expelled from the country; party members were forbidden to belong to a church; and the people as a whole were discouraged from attending services.

The antireligious drive extended to all faiths. The Jews, the Muslims, and the Buddhists were persecuted along with the Christians. After the Revolution the mosques were closed in Central Asia, as were Buddhist temples in southeastern Siberia and Jewish synagogues in various parts of the country.

Outright persecution was shortlived. It strengthened rather than weakened religion. "Religion is like a nail; the harder you hit it the deeper it goes into the wood," a Soviet Minister of Education said in frustration. Furthermore, religious persecution aroused hostility abroad; and once the Communists realized that world revolution was not within sight, they tried to improve their relations with other countries as a matter of survival. The attack on religion took a less direct form. The Constitution of 1936 promised freedom of religious worship. At the same time, however, it recognized "freedom of antireligious propaganda." While religious propaganda was confined to the inside of the church and to the home, antireligious propaganda was spread by the school, the press, and every other means of communication.

During World War II, the Soviet government tried to strengthen popular support by relaxing various restrictions, including those on religious worship. The church, it found, could be put to use to rally believers in time of war (or to preach peace, when it suited Communist policy). Christian teachings improved public morals; and morals, as far as daily relations between people were concerned, were after all as important for a Communist society as for a non-Communist one. Last but not least, the priests, who in Tsarist times had been expected to report to the police "politically untrustworthy" individuals, could be helpful once again.

After the war, antireligious propaganda was resumed. Posters show church bells ringing-in money for the clergy and drunks celebrating religious holidays, "for if it were not for God, they could not drink so much." Little sputniks with friendly faces peer from placards and proclaim: "We have been all

The political "demonstration" has taken the place of the religious procession. The pictures of Communist leaders are carried like the icons of old on a snowy May Day in Leningrad.

through outer space and did not find God." "Humorous" versions ridicule the Bible. Today most churches and synagogues in the Soviet Union are like hollow shells, but the very persistence of antireligious propaganda is proof of the fact that Christianity and Judaism have not been stamped out completely, even though their hold is largely confined to the older generation.

After almost half a century of atheistic propaganda, the churches are attended almost exclusively by old women. If the churches are crowded on great religious holidays, one must remember that only a few churches are open. Young people, when a party gets dull, go out to watch the old-timers prostrate themselves on the stone floor and sometimes break up religious services, whether on instructions from the Communist Youth Organization or "for the fun of it." University students will ask an American visitor, "Do you really believe in God?" with the sort of incredulous curiosity with which one might inquire in the United States if a nuclear physicist still believed in Santa Claus. They cannot understand how an educated person can be so "superstitious."

Yet man is not sufficient unto himself. To a certain extent communism has taken the place of religion in Soviet life. The writings of Marx and Lenin are respected like the "gospel truth" and are spread with missionary zeal and self-sacrifice. The pictures of Communist leaders are carried in political demonstrations like icons in religious processions. In the Palace of Pioneers in Moscow flowers are placed before a large painting of Lenin with the inscription "Lenin lived, Lenin is alive, Lenin will live." Long lines of

Russians daily file past the body of Lenin, which lies embalmed in the mausoleum on Red Square, and view it with deep reverence.

Yet, with time, visions fade and the fervor of the new convert cools. Like the Christian clergy of old, Communist party members uphold basic beliefs and doctrines, though increasingly less dogmatically. The population at large believes in communism the way it once believed in Christianity. It is a way of life in which the people have been raised. They attend meetings and demonstrations; they read and repeat slogans. But with the passing of years their actions and thoughts seem to be becoming routine, and their acceptance of communism appears to be more a matter of habit than of conviction.

EIGHT

THE ARTS

Russian artistic achievements are unevenly known in the West. Russian music and Russian literature are widely appreciated. Russian architecture and Russian painting, on the other hand, are less familiar, partly because they have been less accessible.

ARCHITECTURE

The introduction of Christianity into Kievan Russia in the tenth century molded early Russian architecture. Major buildings were religious in function; and as Christianity had been brought from Byzantium, they were Byzantine in style. Greek architects erected the oldest stone cathedrals and churches, and Greek painters with their Russian students adorned them. Other outside influences, notably Italian, also appeared; but gradually Russian conditions affected the foreign styles, and a national architecture evolved. In Vladimir, about 120 miles east of Moscow, there remain magnificent monuments of this architecture—

twelfth-century churches blending Byzantine, Romanesque, and Russian traditions.

One of the Russian conditions that affected style was the existence of great forests. Blessed with an abundance of lumber, the Russians liked to build out of wood. Wood can be carved readily, and ornate exteriors were common. This style was applied to the stone architecture introduced from abroad. Thus, some of the features of the famous sixteenth-century Cathedral of St. Basil the Blessed in Moscow's Red Square can be traced back directly to wooden architecture.

With the Westernization of Russia, begun by Peter the Great in the eighteenth century, Russian church buildings (as well as Russian palaces) began to resemble their West European counterparts more. The magnificent St. Isaac's Cathedral with its golden dome, for example, would look as much at home in Paris or in Rome as it does in Leningrad.

In secular architecture the style of wooden buildings also influenced the style of early stone construction. Houses and palaces were irregular in shape and often consisted of several units connected by covered passages and stairways. In the new capital of St. Petersburg, founded in 1703, European architects were employed and Russian palaces and public buildings copied the changing styles of Europe. Thus Leningrad is like an architectural museum. The former *Kunstkammer*, Russia's first museum and now the home of the Institute of Ethnography and Anthropology, is an example of a style known as Russian Baroque. The old Winter Palace, formerly the home of the Tsars and now housing the Hermitage Museum, was built in the more decorative Rococo. The Cathe-

dral and Fortress of Peter and Paul, as well as the Twelve Colleges, now Leningrad State University, are in Northern Baroque. The St. Petersburg Stock Exchange, now the Central Naval Museum, and the St. Isaac's Cathedral illustrate a blending of the neoclassic style and Russian tradition.

The Revolution of 1917 was hailed by many architects as an end to tradition. Henceforth the forms and functions of the machine age were to inspire them, and they experimented with forms based on the spiral and the circle. Projects appeared for theaters that looked like electric dynamos. One architect

Buildings like the former Kunstkammer *(on the right) and the Academy of Sciences (on the left) make of Leningrad an architectural museum.*

planned a building in the form of a gigantic steel spiral to house the Communist International. The three meeting rooms, contained within, were designed so that they would rotate once a year, once a week, once a day according to the different councils that were to meet there.

In the late 1920's and early 1930's Moscow was a center of progressive twentieth-century architecture. But as the revolutionary spirit slackened and as experimentation gave way to orthodoxy, "Socialist Realism" was imposed on architecture by the Communist party. Socialist Realism—"the truthful, historically concrete presentation of reality in its revolutionary development"—was to educate the masses ideologically in the spirit of socialism. All architects, therefore, were combined into the Union of Soviet Architects and were restricted to designing buildings in a style which the party approved. The results were as stifling in architecture as in other fields of creative endeavor. The reconstruction of Moscow that began in 1935 produced tall but unimaginative buildings. Marble, bronze, and mosaics were lavished on subway stations, and a number of skyscrapers were erected in the "wedding cake" style. Needless to say, chandeliers in subway stations and marble walls in university buildings were neither economical nor functional. Following the death of Stalin the construction of palace-like subway stations was abandoned, and simpler, more modest buildings were erected.

Today, enormous effort is devoted to public housing. Prefabrication is tried on a large scale. Three-ton exterior wall units, complete with glass in windows, and factory-built living rooms are swung into place by gigantic cranes. In the words of *Life* Magazine:

> This is instant housing. . . . The result is rough, but it's ready; it depends on shortcuts and fantastic new methods. . . . Average time required to assemble a five-story 60-unit prefab apartment building is 18 days. In one experiment, to prove it could be done, Soviet construction engineers completed such a building in 24 hours.
>
> On a scale never matched in any other country, the U.S.S.R.'s new computer-guided prefab factories are turning out apartment house components that fit together like a child's building blocks into simplified universal architectural designs. . . . As the industry refines its techniques, there is a trend toward variety to relieve the

Moscow's Hotel Ukraine, where many foreign tourists stay, is built in the "wedding cake" style of the Stalin period.

monotony. To brighten the completed buildings, colorful stone mosaics are set into exterior wall panels and the size of buildings are beginning to be staggered—from five to 16 stories.[8]

The quality of construction, insulation, and apartment size are still below modern European and American standards. But recent modernization of style as well as of technique hold out the promise for dramatic improvement. The Palace of Meetings in the Kremlin, with its gigantic stage and auditorium, and the Palace of Pioneers in Moscow are symbolic of a new trend in Soviet architecture.

PAINTING

Painting, like architecture, was primarily religious in character until the period of Peter the Great. Greek icons (religious images) and Greek painters were brought to Kievan Russia, and Russian artists produced icons, enamels, mural frescoes, and mosaics in the Byzantine style. Gradually, they assimilated the foreign art; and as the various Russian territories combined, a national style of painting developed. Flat, ornamental, and colorful, this style succeeded in giving to the saints whom it portrayed a remarkable expression of the eyes. They seemed to be looking inwards and beyond, through the worshipper. The Mongol conquest, which gave Russian art a touch of semi-Oriental splendor, did not alter its basically religious direction. The finest icons were painted by Andrei Rublev in fifteenth-century Moscow.

In the second half of the sixteenth century many icon painters from other parts of the country were brought to Moscow to participate in the restoration of the city, which had been devastated by fire. Organized in government workshops as employees of the state rather than of the church, the artists produced more and more secular paintings; they portrayed scenes from Russian history, glorifying princes rather than saints. The reforms of Peter the Great in the eighteenth century further reduced religious influence on Russian art. With a genius for absorbing foreign ideas, Russian artists made Renaissance and other Western influences their own. Only in peasant craft did the native genius flourish unchanged, with the same traditional designs, patterns, and color.

While Russian paintings came to resemble those of the West more and more, their emphasis was different. Less concerned with stylistic and technical innovations—with the means of communication—Russian artists laid greater stress on meaning. Subscribing to the statement that "the true function of art is to explain life and comment on it," Russian painters in the second half of the nineteenth century, like their counterparts and friends in literature, tried to arouse compassion for the common man and thereby improve social conditions. These artists, like the writers, were nationalists. Unlike the upper classes which imitated foreign culture, the artists were concerned with the common man and thus with Russia. The works of Ilya Repin and Vasily Surikov are outstanding examples of this trend in Russian painting.

By the end of the nineteenth century, the photographic detail of Realism was abandoned by many painters in favor of new techniques of expression. Many forms of modern and abstract art, striving to get at the heart of an idea, feeling, or vision without bothering with its outward detail, were first developed

in Russia. With the overthrow of the Tsar and of the Provisional Government in 1917, experimentation accelerated as artists sought revolutionary techniques. But their works could not be readily understood by the general public and seemed to serve no useful social function. This was no time for art for art's sake, Communists argued; and many artists, the Association of Artists of Revolutionary Russia, for example, agreed.

With the consolidation of the Soviet regime and particularly with the dictatorship of Stalin, art, like every other aspect of Russian life, became subject to

Leningrad panorama: the Hermitage (former Winter Palace) on the left, the beacons in the center, the Central Naval Museum (former Stock Exchange) on the right.

state regulation. Leading modern painters such as Vasily Kandinsky and Marc Chagall, who were not willing to subject their art to political restrictions, left the country. Those who remained behind had to paint (and sculpt) according to the principles of Socialist Realism. They were to depict the realities of Soviet life from a Communist point of view in order to inspire the people with the spirit of Soviet socialism. Such work was "realistic" in the sense that it portrayed the subject matter almost photographically. But in the process of selling communism, it idealized Soviet life. Unlike nineteenth-century Realism, which emanated from the artists' souls and resulted in some great works of art, Socialist Realism, decreed by the party, produced paintings and sculptures that resembled billboard advertisements.

The general relaxation of control which followed Stalin's death was felt in art as well. Young Russians sought to obtain books on modern art and tried to experiment on their own. Though they were publicly ridiculed and criticized by Khrushchev and the Soviet press, they were not stifled as in the days of Stalin. With the further relaxation that followed Khrushchev's fall from power, experiments have continued. A new store in Leningrad which sells the works of local artists contains objects that show increasing originality. With the gradual acceptance of modern architecture and modern music, there is hope for somewhat freer expression in art also.

MUSIC

In early times Russian folk music, influenced to some extent by Roman Catholic choir singing, was polyphonic, with two or more distinct melodies combined in one composition. As the Greek Orthodox Church in the Byzantine tradition opposed harmony, Russian folk music and religious music remained separate, without contributing to each other. Consequently, until the introduction of Western music, Russian Church music remained undeveloped, while Russian folk song even thereafter retained its traditional scale and rhythm. Noting that Russian peasants were so used to harmonizing by ear that they would sound well-rehearsed with strangers, one historian observed:

> Russian folk singing is rendered with chesty, whole-

hearted fervor. Immediately striking is the deep bass and heavy alto; both men's and women's voices in Russia seem to have a distinctive, almost raucous depth, perhaps owing to the peculiarities of the Russian language, which develops the lower register. The old, pioneer folk-song hunters felt some surprise that only one or two voices in a women's choral group would be sopranos, and that even they would have to be classified as higher altos. One of the best sources on bygone Russian music . . . published in London in 1671 . . . notes that in Russia "a strenuous voice loseth nothing by its harsh notes. For the Russians love nothing soft or smooth but their women's fat sides." [9]

With the introduction of Western notation, theory, and forms, Russian music was rejuvenated. Applying Western techniques to their ancient traditions of religious and folk music, Russian composers produced works that were at once beautiful and distinct.

It was in the nineteenth century that Russian music, like Russian art and literature, reached its height. Like art and literature, too, it became noted for its realism. In their works, composers sought to portray the people as they actually were. Thus, Modest Musorgsky, in his operas "Boris Godunov" and "Khovanshchina," depicted the common people, without idealization but with sympathy and understanding.

Whereas Alexander Borodin added an Oriental flavor to his music, composers like Peter Tchaikovsky and Nicholas Rimsky-Korsakov turned to Russian folk music and national folklore for inspiration in symphonic as well as operatic productions. While Russian music thus developed a national character, the international language of music allowed a give-and-take in influence. Borodin, for example, influenced the French composers Claude Debussy and Maurice Ravel.

At the end of the nineteenth century and at the

beginning of the twentieth century composers like Vladimir Rebikov turned their backs on traditional forms of harmony, regarding music as the language of emotions, devoid of form, laws, or rules. Among the great experimenters who searched for different means of expression was Igor Stravinsky, a leader rather than a follower of European music. Sergei Prokofiev was another modern composer of world fame; original and

The Palace of Meetings, built on the ancient Kremlin grounds, provides the performing arts with one of the world's largest stages.

dynamic, his music was more melodic than Stravinsky's and could be appreciated by more people.

In music, as in architecture and painting, conformity became the rule after the Communist Revolution. Most leading composers emigrated (Prokofiev only temporarily). Those who remained behind withdrew into themselves or wrote mostly conservative, easy-to-understand music which reflected at times the old Russian love for pageantry in gigantic proportion. The works of Prokofiev, whose training was prerevolutionary, and of such Soviet composers as Dmitry Kabalevsky, Aram Khachaturian, and Dmitry Shostakovich are often played abroad.

In popular music, jazz is much liked by young Russians. In Leningrad, for example, there are a number of jazz groups. Though jazz was banned in the days of Stalin and the Communist party continued to condemn it as degenerate and bourgeois at the time of Khrushchev, Russian youngsters in the 1960's learned to play Western-style popular music and to dance to it. They listened to the Voice of America and taped the latest hits; their knowledge of American and English jazz personalities was remarkable. This is worth mentioning as a postscript to Soviet music, for progressive jazz and American dancing, like modern art, throw off the shackles of tradition and seek free expression.

PERFORMING ARTS

The Russian theater of the late nineteenth century was known for its fine acting. The ideas of Konstantin Stanislavsky, founder and director of the Moscow Art Theater, influenced actors all over the world. Stanislavsky insisted that acting be realistic and that performers relive the part. This has become known everywhere as the "Stanislavsky method." After the Revolution the technique was abandoned as too abstruse for the masses, who now were expected to go to the theater. Overacting was regarded as necessary on the stage and in early Soviet movies. As the education and understanding of the general public increased, more natural acting became desirable. In recent years some Soviet productions of classical plays and some Soviet movies have been marked by sensitive direction and acting. The children's theater and the puppet theater (for adults and children) are highly developed art forms in the Soviet Union.

Russian violinists, pianists, and singers have toured Europe and America with great success. But it is the Russian ballet that is most celebrated. Soviet students, boys as well as girls, follow ballet with as much enthusiasm as American students follow baseball. They know all the leading dancers and shower male and female stars with flowers. Ballets with a Communist message, such as "Spartacus," tend to sacrifice artistic expression to convey meaning clearly to the masses, but such classical ballets as "Swan Lake" or such Soviet ballets as "Stone Flower" are sheer delight. In the U.S.S.R., unlike the United States, ballets are usually performed in their entirety, with a whole evening devoted to one ballet. Elaborate stage setting, which the Russians use masterfully, greatly adds to the effect.

The arts in the Soviet Union have suffered from governmental control. Attempts to use them as vehicles for propaganda have stunted their growth. In painting, where the subject matter was most obvious, the damage has been greatest. In music, where expression could less easily be judged politically, a number of fine works have been composed. As the Soviet Union seeks to impress the world with its cultural achievements, it may try to encourage its artists to experiment somewhat more freely.

NINE

LITERATURE AND THOUGHT

Early Russian literature, like architecture and art, was religious in character and purpose. It consisted primarily of translations of the Scriptures, hymns, and other religious writings from Greek into Old Church-Slavonic. The first significant example of secular literature was *The Song of Igor's Campaign,* an epic poem of approximately the twelfth century. Relating the campaign of a Kievan prince against the Tatars, it conveyed the spirit of the warriors and extolled the virtue of self-sacrifice for Russia. Other early nonreligious writings were the chronicles—historical records compiled by many Russian cities—family precepts, and legal acts. Written for purposes of instruction rather than of entertainment, these early Russian works gave root to the Russian tradition that literature (like architecture and art) be religiously and morally useful.

Side by side with the literature that was written in Church-Slavonic there flourished an oral folk literature of stories, ballads, and songs in the spoken language of the people. This folk literature was not set down on paper until the seventeenth and eighteenth centuries. It reflected Russian mentality better than the Byzantine-weighted written works and was to inspire modern poets and novelists with its freshness of expression, observations, and style.

The Mongol conquest hindered the development of Russian literature, but in the sixteenth century it resumed its growth. The introduction of printing broadened the circle of readers and writers. As the influence of the church weakened, its religious hold on literature loosened; and works set down in the spoken language increased. The reforms of Peter the Great extended to literature. The alphabet was simplified, and all but religious books were printed in the new letters. Yet Peter the Great's efforts at Westernization were confined to the upper classes, who lived and thought differently from the masses. The distinction in thought and even in language that developed resembled the former split between religious and folk expression.

Many writers during the eighteenth century were government officials. They believed that privileges carried with them certain obligations and that it was the duty of noblemen, like themselves, to serve their ruler and people. Regarding themselves as servants of the state, they clung to the traditional view that literature should have a purpose and, like the religious propagandists of old, spread the official beliefs of the day. Western forms and standards dominated Russian works; but important improvements and simplifications in language and style were attained, preparing the way for the great flowering of national literature in the nineteenth century.

Alexander Pushkin, the great Russian poet and literary figure, ushered in the golden age of Russian literature and thought in the brief years of his life (1799-1837). In his marvelous poems, lyrics, novels, stories, and plays, he gave shape to modern literary Russian—clear, direct and musical, free from artificial mannerisms or Church-Slavonic trappings. As one scholar points out: "A poem by Pushkin in Russian creates the impression that what he says could never be said otherwise, that each word fits perfectly, serving as a necessary part of a whole, and that no other words could ever assume a similar function. And still these words are, for the most part, the plain words we use in daily talk." [10]

Pushkin was absolutely natural in his statements and used folk elements of speech in his writing. Although he was an aristocrat, he was an ardent liberal, concerned with the dignity of man. He sympathized with the Decembrists, though his exile precluded his participation in the uprising. Because of his views, he was not allowed by the government to travel abroad. In Pushkin's masterpiece *Eugene Onegin,* a novel in verse, truth emerged victorious over emptiness from loss of faith and conviction. Truth, and the search for truth rather than beauty, became an obsession with Russia's greatest writers. "I have not learned to love my country with my eyes closed, my head bowed, and my mouth shut," Peter Chaadaev wrote in 1837. "I think that one can be useful to one's country only if one sees it clearly; I believe that the age of blind love has passed, and that nowadays one owes one's country the truth. . . ." [11] Unable to lead a free political life in nineteenth-century Russia, intellectuals used literature as a forum for the debate of Russia's mission and character. The possibility of opposing the autocratic government in this way drew leading spirits into literature and filled the pages of Russian novels with social significance.

Michael Lermontov, like Pushkin, was an outstanding poet and died in a duel. Like Pushkin, also, he sympathized with the Decembrists whose revolt had been crushed in 1825. He even foretold the end of the monarchy: "The dark day of Russia will come when the crown of the Tsars will fall, when the mob, oblivious of its former allegiance, will spread death and blood far and wide."[12] In his poetry and prose Lermontov condemned the injustices of life and the emptiness of society. He searched for moral justification and truth, for the reason of being. Nicholas Gogol in his comedy *The Inspector General* and in the novel *Dead Souls* laid bare the shortcomings and injustices of Russia's social order. Gogol's ridicule of the bureaucracy and condemnation of serfdom and of absolute government delighted the liberals until he had a change of heart and, becoming deeply involved in religion, defended the old institutions. The novelist and playwright Ivan Turgenev realistically described the life of the common people in his famous collection of stories *Notes of a Hunter* (known also as *A Sportsman's Notebook*). In his novel *Fathers and Children* he portrayed the rise of a new, radical generation with a strong faith in science and material things and little else, and he examined the conflict between the new and the old. In his search for truth he offended conservatives and radicals alike.

Feodor Dostoyevsky is best known for his novels *The Brothers Karamazov* and *Crime and Punishment*, in which he used a psychological approach. As a young man he had become involved with a group of Utopian Socialists and had been condemned to death. His sentence had been commuted to four years' imprisonment at the very last moment, as he stood on the scaffold. The shock of mounting the scaffold deeply affected him. His first novel, *Poor People,* had examined social conditions. Now his search for truth shifted to the state of mind, psychology, and the groping for God. In his novel *The Possessed,* he prophesied a revolution in which men would turn their backs on God and seek happiness in complete equality and material possessions. Dostoyevsky appreciated the weighty burden of freedom, which confronted man with choice after choice. He did not think that man could be free and happy, so heavy was the responsibility of deciding, for example, whether or not to believe in God. Yet Dostoyevsky remained an advocate of freedom, seeing in freedom the divine spark of God.

Ivan Goncharov examined the upbringing of the ruling class and found it wanting. In his novel *Oblomov* he described the Russian nobility as weak and unable to provide active leadership. Anton Chekhov in his short stories and plays portrayed all classes of Russian society "with laughter through tears." He described the decay of the landowning aristocracy and the inactivity of many intellectuals.

Russia's most celebrated novelist was Count Leo Tolstoy. His *War and Peace* and *Anna Karenina* are among the greatest works of fiction in the world. In the former he dealt with the Russian campaign against Napoleon and examined the importance of individual persons in the course of history. In the latter he exposed the prejudices of aristocratic society. A country gentleman and one-time army officer, Tolstoy described life in the country and on the battlefield with remarkable realism. Filled with deep affection for the common people, he tried to improve their harsh living conditions by word and deed. At the same time he identified himself with the common people, worked in the fields, and often wore peasant clothing.

Searching for the meaning of life, Tolstoy eventually became obsessed with the worthlessness of fame and worldly success. He gave up writing fiction and denied the value of the great novels he had created. He turned to religious and philosophical works, in which he criticized the state, society, and the organized church. Consequently excommunicated by the church, he was spared imprisonment only because of his enormous popularity, lest he become a martyr for his ideas. While he attacked the church, Tolstoy did not reject religion. On the contrary, as he wrote in 1904, after the outbreak of the Russo-Japanese War:

> The evil from which men of our time are suffering is produced by the fact that the majority live without . . . that religion which establishes the relation of man to the All, to God, and, therefore, gives a general higher direction to all human activity. . . . This evil which is leading men to inevitable destruction has manifested itself with special power in our time, because . . . having directed all efforts to discoveries and improvements principally in the sphere of technical knowledge, men of our time have developed in themselves enormous power over the forces of nature; but . . . have used it for the satisfaction of their lowest and most animal propensities. . . . Man has no choice; he must be the slave of the most unscrupulous and insolent among slaves, or else the servant of God, because for man there is only one way of being free—by uniting his will with the will of God.[13]

Tolstoy's religious outlook made a deep impression on spiritual leaders throughout the world. His outspoken opposition to war in particular influenced the nonviolence of Mahatma Gandhi. The morally instructive character of Tolstoy's later works was in the tradition of Russia's early literature. Writing with an educational purpose and sacrificing his own art in order to spread his ideas, he also foreshadowed the thinking of Soviet authors.

Shoulder to shoulder with the poets and novelists, literary critics and political philosophers voiced their demands for social justice and tried to uplift the common people. Aware of the wide gulf that existed between the educated classes and the downtrodden masses, a group of intellectuals, some of them noblemen, felt guilty. They believed it their duty, therefore, to go to the common people and, living among them, to educate them. As they had little opportunity in autocratic Russia to promote political and social reforms, they were greatly frustrated. Therefore in their thought and talk they leaned toward revolutionary extremism.

Among the intellectuals there were apostles of freedom who realized the importance of individual liberty. "Individual liberty is the supreme good; on this basis alone the true will of the people can express itself," Alexander Herzen declared.[14] But there were others in the nineteenth century, as in the twentieth, who did not think that individual freedom was necessary for revolutionary justice. Their search for truth and justice was emotional; it was based on faith in the peculiar character and mission of Russia. So strong indeed was the patriotic vision of some prerevolutionary Russian writers that in spite of the actual conditions in their country they believed, like their Soviet successors, that the future belonged to Russia—that the Russian people were destined to save mankind.

The outbreak of revolution in 1917 at first inspired writers as it had artists and musicians. The ferocity of the civil war and the threat posed by foreign intervention found the poet in the midst of the struggle. As Vladimir Mayakovsky proclaimed:

Polish Commanders
    Branded our backs with
        Five-pointed stars.
Mamontov's bands
    Buried us alive
        Up to our necks.
The Japanese
    Burned us in the fireboxes
        of locomotives
    And poured lead and tin
        into our mouths.
They all roared:
    "Abjure!"
But from our burning throats
    Only three words came:
    "Long
      Live
        Communism!" [15]

A somewhat calmer but no less determined poetic exhortation was composed by Valery Bryusov.

Fresh are the dews, Come brothers and sing:
no better time for a scythe to swing.
    We lift eight shoulders in a row
    and we mow, we mow, we mow, we mow.
The whistling of bullets has now begun

and up is that redhaired god the sun
over the meadows. Let fear all go.
The day won't wait for us: so we mow.
Across the fields to the slope of the hill
go barefoot down, go freshly still.
No mercy will the bullets show
and under the hail of lead we mow.
Watch how we do it, you milksops there,
while wasps of bullets rasp in our hair.
Wolves after reindeer, the bullets aren't slow,
but our ancient task we perform and mow.
Hey for the sailors who know no fear!
Straight for the cliff-face our course we steer.
With Russian joy, we none of us know
if it's pass or fall, but like wind we mow.
And if we come through, no questions allowed!
An eight-voice song now and make it loud!
Maybe we'll all stretch dead in a row
but the meadow of green to the end we'll mow.[16]

But the horrors of civil war also aroused compassion, and some writers pointed to the senselessness of killing, to the fact that in death there were no Whites or Reds, only men. As Marina Tsvetayeva wrote:

They all lie in a row—
No line between them.
Look: soldiers!
Who's ours? Who's theirs?
He was white and now he's red—
The blood reddened him.
He was red and now he's white—
Death whitened him.[17]

During the civil war many intellectuals emigrated. Novelists like Ivan Bunin and religious philosophers like Nicholas Berdyayev continued to write abroad in Russian. Bunin received the Nobel prize for literature in 1933. Younger men like Vladimir Nabokov began to write in other languages also. Some of the emigrants returned to Russia. Aleksei Tolstoy, for example, went back to the U.S.S.R. in 1923 to become a popular novelist. He dealt with historical themes from a Soviet point of view. Other writers, like Maxim Gorky, who had made a name for themselves before the Revolution continued their literary activity in the Soviet Union. Gorky depicted the hard life of the common people in a natural and often depressing way and contributed to the development of Socialist Realism.

Literature, like the arts, witnessed a great deal of experimentation in the 1920's. Some authors tried to adjust prerevolutionary forms of expression to new subjects and feelings; others searched for new styles as well as new topics. The civil war was the setting for many works. Foundries, mines, and machines also became popular subjects as proletarian poets and novelists who had not written before took up the pen. This was the period of the New Economic Policy, and the government relaxed its control and encouraged individual initiative in literature as well as economics.

In the 1930's the Communist party began to stifle experimentation, demanding order and purpose in all areas of life, including literature and the arts. No longer were poetic feeling and inspiration alone enough. Writers, like everyone else, were to work in the building of a Communist state. Not only were their topics to be relevant to the needs of the people but their style was to be simple so that it could be understood by the masses. Writing was to be positive, to inspire the people. Michael Sholokhov, whose *And*

Quiet Flows the Don, a book about Cossack life during World War I and the civil war, became the most popular novel in the Soviet Union, had to interrupt his work on it in order to turn out a novel about the collectivization of agriculture *(Virgin Soil Upturned).*

As Stalin's hold over the country tightened, criticism of the regime or of life in the Soviet Union became increasingly difficult and dangerous. The works of such talented writers as Michael Zoshchenko and Vera Inber, who satirized the new society with marvelous humor, were repeatedly suppressed. Other authors who failed to curb their spirits and remained true to themselves rather than to Socialist Realism were deported or sent to forced labor camps and insane asylums; some were shot. Vladimir Mayakovsky, who had written the enthusiastic poem quoted above, committed suicide.

The creative genius of the writers was not destroyed completely. Here and there sensitive poems and beautiful stories appeared in print, and poems and stories that could not be published were circulated in manuscript form and passed on by word of mouth. Poetry, which had always been popular in Russia, was particularly suited for oral recitation. It was brief and relatively vague. During the Second World War many writers were put into the field as war correspondents. While this limited their output of fiction, they were exposed to common human emotions and again became interested in basic human feelings and values. Poetry formed a natural vehicle for the expression of their personal sentiments.

The political relaxation that followed Stalin's death had its counterpart in literature. In fact, one referred to the new political climate as "The Thaw,"

A statue of Pushkin, Russia's greatest poet, stands in front of the Russian Museum.

after the novelette by Ilya Ehrenburg. Ehrenburg mentioned in this work the political arrests and banishments of the 1930's, a topic until then passed over in silence, and questioned the artistic worth of officially approved art. While such great writers as Konstantin Paustovsky, Michael Sholokhov, and Konstantin Simonov remained guarded in their portrayal of contemporary life, novelists like Vladimir Dudintsev *(Not by Bread Alone)* and poets like Yevgeny Yevtushenko exposed the imperfections of Soviet society. In the novel *Doctor Zhivago* the noted poet Boris Pasternak portrayed the destruction of an intellectual who remained detached from the revolutionary events around him as he clung to the traditional values of Christianity and humanity.

An artist, to be an artist, must first of all be true to himself. As Pushkin had written in 1836:

> To be dependent on a monarch or the people—
> Is it not all the same? God bless them, anyhow.
> To serve and please oneself alone, to be resolved that
> Not conscience, intellect, nor neck shall ever bow
> Before authority or livery; but freely
> To wander here and there, as fancy may take flight,
> Rejoicing in the holy radiance of nature,
> The pulses thrilling with a keen and pure delight
> Before the arts of men, the works of inspiration—
> —That's happiness! Those are our veritable rights—[18]

It was in this tradition that young Yevtushenko, who was enormously popular among the Soviet youth, wrote in a poem entitled "Consider Me a Communist!":

> There are many who dislike me,
> Reproaching me for this and that. . . .

Russians are eager readers of modern and classical literature. Books are cheap and sell rapidly.

Their looks of hate and malice
I feel behind my back.
But I am pleased with all of this,
And I am proud because
They cannot break me down
Or force me to my knees.[19]

Khrushchev, who then headed the Soviet government, was displeased with the new trend. He reprimanded the authors for approaching the tasks of literature and art "in a mistaken, distorted manner," showing the bad sides of Soviet life "counter to Leninist principles concerning the approach of the party and the government to problems of literature and life." Boris Pasternak, whose novel *Doctor Zhivago* had been smuggled out and published abroad only, was prevented from accepting the Nobel prize in literature.

Shortly after finding it impossible to accept the Nobel prize, Pasternak wrote a poem which is a monument to those who, like himself, have refused to sell their souls.

Lost, like a cornered beast, I'm lost.
Somewhere people live in light,
Joy, and freedom. As for me,
I am hounded, trapped outright.

In a forest by a pond
I am like a levelled tree.
There is no escape. No matter.
Let the hunt and hunters be!

What the vile offence I've dared?
Am I a bandit out of hand,

I who made the world weep tears
Over beauty in my land?

None the less, I still believe,
Though I feel my death is near,
That the soul of men's goodwill
Will defeat all hate and fear.[20]

While Khrushchev tried to gag Pasternak, he explicitly approved the publication in the U.S.S.R. of Alexander Solzhenitsyn's long story *One Day in the Life of Ivan Denisovich,* which exposed life in a Stalinist concentration camp. This work was a milestone in postwar Russian literature, not only because it revealed the evils of a period in Soviet history but also because it was written in the old realistic, humanist tradition, free of the falseness of Socialist Realism. It reminds one of Dostoyevsky's *Memoirs from the Dead House,* which described Siberian prison life in Tsarist times. The further relaxation of dictatorial controls following Khrushchev's removal from office has seen the appearance of an increasing number of works whose publication would have been inconceivable in the 1930's or 1940's. When Michael Sholokhov was awarded the Nobel prize in 1965 for "the artistic power and integrity with which, in his epic of the Don, he has given creative expression to a historic phase in the history of the Russian people," the Soviet government allowed him to accept it.

This does not mean that there is free expression in the Soviet Union, nor that the critical writers are anti-Communist. There is serious disagreement among the authors themselves as to how much freedom to seek. Their target is the corruption of the system, rather than the system itself. Yet any criticism remains dangerous, for no one knows how the next dictator or "collective leadership" will react to their writing.

Today Soviet authors are content to write for the general public. They do not strive for complicated forms that only few can understand. But they believe that with the spread of education the people are ready for a higher level of expression and that henceforth simplicity can be of a different kind. In the words of Semyon Kirsanov:

> There's a desire
>   a dream. We think:
> O to be simple, simply good,
> simply simple
>   as food and drink,
> simple as tracks that thread a wood,
> simple
>   as a pipe at play,
> an easy pleasing unqueazy mode,
> simple
>   as yellow stacks of hay
> or a bare signpost by the road,
> simple
>   as a straight-drawn line
> as 2 by 2 is always 4.
> O such simplicity may be fine
> but what on earth will it do for you?
> No,
>   I want simplicity
> that's like the harvester's
>   revealed
> to him who drives it deftly free
> across the thick heat-flickering field,
> the choice
>   where crossing roads abound

and one is right and other wrong,
simple
as the solution found
for tasks that teased your wits for long,
simple
as figures which, when added,
into the Five Years Plan all gather,
simple
as my brown eye that's made
of cells in millions come together,
the sky
where stars profusely sprawl
as simple as a nuclear section
or Chinese speech that's clear to all
who turn to China with affection.
Simplicity
doesn't linger, plainly
marking time, but far it ranges.
It's gone to school to study again
and with the people it grows and changes.[21]

TEN

FOREIGN RELATIONS

In 1917, when the Communists seized control of the government, Russia was still at war with Germany. Lenin was more concerned about maintaining his leadership in Russia than he was about the "capitalist war" that was being waged between the Allies and the Central Powers, and he made a separate peace with Germany. The price was high in terms of Russian territory lost, but Lenin believed that soon revolution would sweep away all national boundaries and communism would rule the globe. For this reason and in order to get a fresh start in foreign policy as in other areas, Lenin also repudiated all the treaties and debts of Tsarist Russia.

The Communists aroused Allied hostility further by confiscating foreign property without compensation, by demanding reparations for the Allied intervention during the Russian civil war, and by publishing the secret correspondence and agreements between the Tsarist government and the Allied Powers. In fact, the Communists actively worked to overthrow the governments of Russia's former allies from within by encouraging their citizens to revolt. To further the victory of international communism, the Communists in 1919 formed the Comintern (the Communist International), an organization of national Communist parties controlled by Moscow. At the Second Comintern Congress in 1920, the delegates of the various countries pledged themselves "to put up an armed struggle for the overthrow of the international bourgeoisie." [22]

When the working classes of the world did not revolt, the Soviet leaders were forced to reexamine their position. Exhausted by World War I and the civil war, Russia could not go to war with the other powers. If the Communists wished to maintain the beachhead that they had secured in Russia, they must find means of peaceful coexistence. This did not mean that they abandoned their objective of world revolution; it meant a temporary change in tactics. In the 1920's the Soviet regime concluded treaties, first with the border states which had been part of the old empire (Estonia, Lithuania, Latvia, Finland, and Poland), then with other powers, notably Germany, England, China, and Japan. The United States did not recognize the Soviet government until 1933.

Soviet relations with Germany and China were particularly close for a number of years because both Germany and China were embittered by Allied decisions at the Paris Peace Conference that ended World War I, and like Russia, both were in need of friends. In her treaty with Germany (the Treaty of Rapallo, 1922) Russia gave up her war reparations claims against Germany in return for Germany's cancellation of Tsarist debts. The treaty also opened the door for close economic and political ties.

When the Western democracies failed to give support to the Chinese Nationalists in their struggle to unify the country, the U.S.S.R. in the 1920's sent hundreds of military advisers and Communist agents to help the Nationalists gain control of the country. Communist efforts to dominate the Chinese revolutionary movement backfired, however, when the Nationalists expelled the men who had helped them to power.

Russian interest in China, it should be added, was motivated by another factor as well. Marxists believed that the prosperity of the capitalist world depended on the exploitation of the colonial and semi-colonial countries. Thus a revolution in China, even a nationalist one, if it drove out the British and other capitalist exploiters would undermine the strength and prosperity of the capitalist states at home. Soviet activity in China in the 1920's thus was concerned primarily with the impact of events on Europe; the stirring up of revolution in Asia due to interest in Asia itself generally did not take place until after World War II.

From the Soviet point of view the world was divided into two rival camps, the camp of capitalism and the camp of socialism. But while the Soviet Union alone represented the camp of socialism for decades, she did not deal with the camp of capitalism as a whole. Once she entered upon diplomatic relations, she decided to do so more or less in the manner of capitalist states and worked now with one state, now with another, to establish a balance of power. Germany seemed the first natural ally; France and England appeared as the main antagonists.

But Communist policy in Germany in the late

1920's and early 1930's was as unsuccessful as the policy in China. Instead of voting with the Social Democrats against the Nazis (National Socialists), the Communists voted with the Nazis to bring about the fall of the Social Democratic government. The Communists believed that Hitler's rise to power would play into their hands. They thought that within a month after Hitler had taken over, the German working class would rally to the Communist cause. Instead, Hitler destroyed the Communist party.

The rise and expansion of fascist Japan and Nazi Germany forced a reappraisal in Soviet policy. In 1934 the Soviet Union became a member of the League of Nations. Heretofore she had regarded the League as a capitalist agency of imperialism and had expected the richest capitalist countries to go to war with each other. Now she looked upon it as a means of collective security. In France and elsewhere, Communists were ordered to collaborate with Socialists in a so-called "Popular Front" to block the extreme conservatives and fascists. In 1935 the U.S.S.R. signed a pact of mutual aid and assistance with France in case of attack by a third power. A similar treaty was concluded with Czechoslovakia, with the qualification that the other power would help if France also helped.

Soviet Russia reestablished diplomatic relations with China in 1932. She sold the Manchurian railroad to the Japanese puppet state of Manchukuo to remove a major source of friction with Japan. As Japanese aggression against China continued, the Chinese Communists joined with the Chinese Nationalists in common opposition, and China and the Soviet Union signed a nonaggression pact in 1937. Soviet arms and advisers were sent to China. Soviet foreign policy in the 1920's and 1930's was defensive; Soviet diplomats and Communist parties made common cause with other countries and parties to protect the security of the U.S.S.R.

But for the moment France and England were unwilling openly to oppose fascism and to collaborate with Soviet efforts to halt German, Italian, and Japanese expansion. In Spain, in 1936-1938, the Soviet Union vainly aided the Popular Front forces against the German- and Italian-backed legions of General Francisco Franco. Along her Manchurian borders, she singlehandedly repulsed Japanese attacks in 1937-1939. In 1938, at the time of the Munich Conference, the U.S.S.R. appeared willing to aid Czechoslovakia if the Western powers did also; but neither England nor France was prepared to stand up to Hitler. While England and France mistrusted the Soviet Union, which had never ceased trying to subvert their governments, the Soviet Union became increasingly suspicious of England and France, believing that they wanted to set Hitler against her. By the time England and France were ready to collaborate with the Soviet Union, she had decided to cooperate (at least temporarily) with Nazi Germany.

By the Nazi-Soviet agreement of August, 1939, Poland and much of Eastern Europe were divided between Germany and the U.S.S.R. The Soviet Union also tried to establish domination over Finland and went to war with that country. For this action she was expelled from the League of Nations in December, 1939. But when Hitler, who had started World War II with his attack on Poland following the Nazi-Soviet agreement, suddenly invaded also the U.S.S.R. in June of 1941, the Soviet Union was thrown back into the

Allied camp. Desperately in need of each other's support, the British and the Soviets signed a mutual assistance pact; and American lend-lease shipments were sent to the U.S.S.R.

The Germans penetrated deeper into Russian territory than they had in World War I and devastated a large part of the country. During the war Stalin's emphasis on nationalism, a let-up in antireligious agitation in the U.S.S.R., the Soviet Union's acceptance of the Atlantic Charter, which promised freedom and self-determination to all countries, and Soviet signing of the United Nations Declaration misled many Westerners into believing that Stalin had changed his outlook. He had not. At the wartime conferences of Teheran (December, 1943), Yalta (February, 1945), and Potsdam (August, 1945) Stalin presented to the Americans and English the appearance of a nationalist. As he discussed with them territorial concessions and readjustments, he assumed the posture of a Russian rather than that of a Communist. The Comintern, which was dedicated to the overthrow of "capitalist" governments, was abolished as a gesture of cooperation.

Although the Soviet Union and the United States collaborated in the war against Germany and Japan, they had different long-range goals. The United States wished to see Europe reconstructed along more or less traditional lines, with the United Nations Organization (an improved version of the League of Nations) smoothing, if not regulating, the course of international relations. The United States expected Europe to maintain a balance of power within itself and planned to withdraw from direct involvement on the continent as soon as possible. The Soviet Union, on the other hand, was determined once and for all to prevent invasion of her ravaged land. She sought to secure her borders by establishing friendly (and to her that meant Communist) governments in Eastern Europe. But while the setting up of such Communist governments seemed a matter of national security to the Soviet Union, to Americans it appeared to be imperialist expansion and a direct threat to the independence of Europe. With Germany and Italy defeated and the Western Allies completely exhausted, the United States assumed the burden of protecting Europe, an act which, of course, seemed hostile from the Soviet point of view. Since practically all power, for the time being, was concentrated in American and Russian hands, the two superpowers found themselves in direct opposition. As they tried to outmaneuver each other, they became involved in a "cold war" (in contrast with the hot war that had just ended).

The struggle for supremacy between the United States and her allies on one hand and the Soviet Union and the other Communist states on the other spread across the globe. Not only did the defeat of Japan remove the major obstacle to Russian expansion in Asia, but the break-up of the large Western colonial empires and the emergence of weak, inexperienced, and underdeveloped states provided new opportunities for revolutionary agitation.

At Western request the Soviet Union had entered the Pacific theater in 1945 (just before the end of the war, but within the promised time period). Thus, when the war ended, Soviet armies and Communist partisan fighters were in strategic positions for supporting Communist uprisings in both Asia and Europe. The defeat of Germany and Japan and the

Political demonstrations harness popular support for the government's foreign policy. On the flag the boy holds, the banner of East Germany appears alongside that of the Soviet Union.

exhaustion of the Allies left the Communists with relatively little opposition. In Greece the Communists tried to seize power but failed. In Yugoslavia and Albania they succeeded more or less on their own. In Rumania, Bulgaria, Hungary, Poland, and Czechoslovakia Soviet armies supported Communist takeovers. Sealed off from the West by an "Iron Curtain," the people were isolated from capitalist countries. They could read only Communist newspapers and were not allowed to travel abroad freely. In China and Indo-China, as in Yugoslavia, the Communists came to power through their leading position in the wartime resistance movements. In Korea, as in Poland, they were installed by Russian troops. Elsewhere in Asia, Communists sought to use popular opposition to the return of the Westerners, driven out by the Japanese during the war, as a means of gaining public support. A Communist Information Bureau (Cominform), established in 1947 in place of the old Comintern, coordinated Communist efforts throughout the world. (It was disbanded in 1956.)

The cold war was marked in Europe in 1948 by the Soviet blockade of Berlin, which lay deep within the Soviet zone of Germany, and by the American airlift, which broke the blockade. The Warsaw Pact of 1955 sought to counteract the North Atlantic Pact of the Western powers by unifying command of the Communist states in Europe. In Asia the Communist offensive was highlighted by the invasion of South Korea by a strong North Korean army in 1950. Though the North Korean armies and the Chinese who came to their support were driven back by a predominantly American United Nations force, North Korea remained in Communist hands. In Vietnam in the 1960's

Communist infiltration from North Vietnam to South Vietnam proceeded less openly; as the Communists scattered through the countryside, they were more difficult to oppose. American involvement in the defense of Vietnam against Communist domination kept Soviet-American relations tense.

American sympathy for the U.S.S.R. in her heroic defense against Nazi aggression had been quickly dispelled after the war by Soviet expansion and by Western realization that Stalin's regime had not really changed. Khrushchev was willing to modify the Soviet position, to make peace in Korea, and to talk about peaceful coexistence of different social systems (but not of different ideologies). He allowed a cultural exchange of scholars and artists with the United States and with other capitalist countries in the hope of impressing the West with Soviet cultural achievements. Yet his attempt to gain strategic advantage over the United States by secretly installing offensive missiles in Communist Cuba in 1962, halted only by the bold stand of President John F. Kennedy, showed that Soviet objectives had not changed.

The emergence of a strong Communist China complicated Soviet foreign affairs. The Chinese Communists had come to power in their country primarily by their own effort; and once they were firmly established, they refused to take orders from Moscow. Turning the antiwhite feeling in the former colonial and semicolonial countries to their advantage, they tried to grab revolutionary leadership in Asia and Africa from Russian hands. A triangular struggle for control of the populous and strategic regions developed between the Soviet Union, China, and the United States. Communist China, with its enormous manpower in Asia, advocated the most aggressive policy, threatening to engage in large-scale land warfare. The Soviet Union, whose industries were more vulnerable to atomic attack, sought to avoid a military confrontation with the United States which might well lead to mutual destruction. Instead the Soviet Union proposed to "bury" capitalism by economic competition and by the support of local revolutions and limited wars of "national liberation."

In the struggle for influence, if not control, the Soviet Union, like the United States and China, gave foreign aid in money, goods, and technical advisers. Richer than China but poorer than the United States, the Soviet Union built factories and dams and furnished products on a loan or trade basis rather than as outright gifts. In the conflict for the minds of men in Asia the Soviet Union had the advantage of opposing the established order with its many injustices, while the United States, in an attempt to halt subversion, tended to become identified with the governments in power. The demand for land redistribution voiced by the Communists was as strong a political weapon in Asia as it had been in Russia during the Revolution. Furthermore, the Communists argued with some success that the Russian (or Chinese) experiences were more applicable to the problems of the underdeveloped countries than were those of the United States and that only a planned economy and firm government control could achieve quick industrialization.

As before, Soviet foreign policy is rooted in Marxism-Leninism. This does not mean that Soviet diplomats believe every slogan they mouth or that every step is rigidly in line with Marxist writings. It does mean that the general worldview of Soviet statesmen is Marxist and that their actions are dictated by the Marxist interpretation of history. While Western diplomats deal with situations as they arise, Soviet diplomats are inclined to take a long-range approach. They believe that the future is theirs; they are confident that capitalism cannot last. At no time have they abandoned the concept of the class struggle; peaceful coexistence to them is the continuation of the class struggle by means other than international war.

Soviet strategy has shifted with changing conditions. At first ideology and world revolution were expected to lead to the downfall of capitalism. Then, when revolutions failed to materialize, expansion by the Soviet Union was regarded as a means toward world revolution. The Communists did not hesitate to collaborate with non-Communist movements if by doing so they could strengthen the influence of the U.S.S.R.

Traditional diplomacy proceeded on the assumption that a given world order was accepted by everyone and that merely a certain adjustment or reshuffling of territory or power was desired. There were rules by which states abided. The Communist Revolution of 1917 changed international relations fundamentally, as the Soviet leaders refused to recognize and abide by the old rules. In response, it should be added, Western nations isolated the Soviet Union and did not apply the provisions of international law to her.

Neither the Soviet Union nor the Western powers observe normal international restraints in dealing with each other. Having denounced bourgeois norms of international law and diplomacy, the Soviets feel free to violate them. While conventional diplomacy sought agreement, revolutionary diplomacy used conferences and agreements as means to other ends and pursued what has been called "a diplomacy of civil war."

Russian expansion during and after World War II was not necessarily related to Marxism-Leninism. Another Russian government might well have done the same to counteract the spread of American and other Western influence following the defeat of Germany and Japan. Marxism-Leninism contributed to Soviet expansion in the sense that Communists were convinced that capitalists were mortal enemies and that everything had to be done to forestall Western expansion as a matter of survival. Marxism-Leninism, furthermore, gained converts to the Soviet cause in foreign countries and thereby aided Russian expansion. Yet revolution increasingly became a technique more than an objective. The preservation and extension of Soviet power, rather than the spread of communism, became the immediate, if not the ultimate, goal of the U.S.S.R.

ELEVEN

LIVING CONDITIONS

The countryside that the traveler in the Soviet Union sees from the train is picturesquely rustic. Charming as the little wooden houses and the horse-drawn carts on the dirt roads appear in passing, they offer a hard life for the village resident. The prospect of assignment to rural communities distresses most university students. They strive, if possible, to remain in large cities, which are the nerve centers of Soviet society. But generally they cannot receive permission to live in such places as Leningrad or Moscow without a job opening, and even then only if housing is available.

In the years following the Revolution of 1917 hunger stalked the land, and the people were dressed in rags. The terrors and privations of World War II left their mark on the 1940's and 1950's. The enormous task of reconstruction and concentration on heavy industry and arms production continued to be a crushing burden on the populace. Since the death of Stalin, greater attention has been paid to the needs of the consumer; and living conditions have improved markedly.

The average urban housewife is still without a refrigerator and spends a great deal of time standing in line to do her daily shopping, but in the large cities food is plentiful and people no longer need to go hungry. The cost of staples like potatoes and bread are kept low by the government, but meat, chicken, and fresh vegetables are expensive. A Soviet family can eat more cheaply than an American family if it sticks to a simple diet; its food bills would be higher were it to buy as much meat and poultry.

While the means of production, such as factories, are owned by the state, the individual may possess personal property such as furniture, television sets, and automobiles. The supply of consumer goods is still far smaller than the demand, and the waiting list for the purchase of such products as cars is extremely long. Crowded living conditions, furthermore, leave little space to store things. But the increase in production of consumer goods and a lowering in cost of many items are bringing greater comfort and pleasures within reach of the average person.

Communists are materialists in the sense that they believe that social, psychological, or historical phenomena should be viewed in terms of physical or material causes rather than in terms of spiritual or ethical causes. They are *not* materialists in the sense of giving undue importance to material interests. They put less emphasis on the standard of living and material acquisitions and comforts than Americans do. The fact that they woo the support of the hungry in their rise to power by promising bread cannot be regarded as undue materialism.

The Soviet Union does not have a classless society. Industrialization on a large scale and national

Kvas, a nonalcoholic fermented beverage made from rye, is a popular Russian drink.

planning could not be left in the hands of workers and peasants. Specialists were needed. A new class of managers and executives developed and grew in numbers and importance as machines and plans became increasingly complex. With time the Soviet executives began to resemble increasingly their prerevolutionary and foreign colleagues in dress, manners, and working conditions.

In addition to the managers and executives, who draw much higher salaries than ordinary workers, there are other privileged groups in Soviet society—military officers, cosmonauts, party officials, professors, lawyers, doctors, writers, painters, actors, and dancers—some of whom receive relatively large apartments, summer cottages, and the use of cars in addition to their pay.

Next in the social structure of the state come the white-collar workers, who sit at their old-fashioned desks in countless offices and institutions writing with their nibbed pens and calculating on their abacuses or on little hand-cranked adding machines. They differ little in appearance from the clerks who shuffled papers before the Revolution.

The workers are next on the social scale, though in theory they are the most important group in the state. Their earnings vary greatly according to their education; skilled workers receive far more than unskilled laborers. Even the highest paid workers are much worse off than leading members of the privileged groups, however.

The peasants remain at the bottom of the scale, with poorer educational facilities in the countryside than in the cities and, consequently, less opportunity for self-improvement. Although the majority of peasants supported the Revolution in order to obtain land, the Communists, once in power, permitted peasants individual use of land for only a short time; then they abolished private agriculture. Joining the individual farms into collectives and state farms, the Communists sought to achieve the mass production common in industry. On the collective farms there are men in key positions who are well off, but the life of most families is harder than that of their city cousins. Mechanization of agriculture is as yet uneven, and nearly half of the Soviet Union's working force is tied to the soil.

The social divisions in the Soviet Union are less pronounced than those that existed in Tsarist Russia. There is now no hereditary ruling class, though the elite still tries to pass privileges on to its children. But an American visitor will find the Russians more class-conscious than his own countrymen. There is less socializing between Russian officers and enlisted men, between Russian bosses and their employees, and between Russian professors and their students than between their counterparts in the United States. The formality that exists in Russian life between superiors and subordinates is softened by the use of the traditional semiformal address of *imia otchestvo*—one's given name plus the patronymic or father's name (for example, Aleksandr Gregoryevich or Aleksandr, son of Gregor; Aleksandra Aleksandrovna or Aleksandra, daughter of Aleksandr.) With the given name reserved only for friends and the surname used in official dealings, the *imia otchestvo* bridges the gap and eases human relations.

If the inhabitants of Leningrad and Moscow seem spruced up today in comparison with the early 1960's, so, too, are the cities themselves. Not only are apartment dwellings multiplying but modern design is coming to the fore. The Palace of Meetings in the Kremlin and the new Palace of Pioneers in Moscow are symbolic of the direction which Soviet architecture has taken recently. It will require many years to overcome the belated start, however. Although modern building projects are springing up everywhere, living conditions remain overcrowded. In apartment houses and in communal dormitories Russians live in close quarters. Thus the newlyweds in a Soviet novel rejoice as they move into a one-room apartment of their own.

It is the lack of privacy in Soviet life that bothers a foreign resident most. Aware that his room may be "bugged" and that his mail may be read by government agents, if not by his roommate, he finds himself fair game for criticism everywhere. Total strangers may come up to him, particularly if they mistake him for a Russian, and tell him that he should not wear a winter cap with a fall coat or that he does not eat enough bread with his meal. Coming upon a husband and wife quarreling in the street, passers-by will take sides and engage in noisy debate.

Yet Russians have a way of creating privacy where none seems to exist to the outsider. Not only do they keep political objections to themselves but they ignore each other much of the time. For example, acquaintances are frequently not introduced or mentioned to each other. If one of several occupants of a room has a visitor, he may not introduce him to his roommates. It may be fear of political involvement; it may be sheer necessity, for if everyone sharing a room would share his friends, no one would have time to do anything else. Russian students complain that

The old kerchief tied in a new way marks off the modern girl from the old-fashioned "babushkas."

their American roommates say "hello" and "good bye" whenever they come and go. Why not just once, in the morning and in the evening?

In their togetherness, Russians make less fuss about sex than Americans. Some dormitories are mixed, men and women sharing the same floor (but they have separate rooms and separate toilet facilities). This does not mean that their relations are more intimate; they are more comradely. Women are accepted as fellow workers more or less on an equal basis. They do heavy, manual labor and are active in the medical field. Most doctors in the Soviet Union are women.

Some early revolutionaries advocated freedom from family and freedom from marriage, and for a number of years marriage and divorce became a mere formality. Gradually the state came to pose as the protector of the family, however, and obtaining a divorce is now more difficult in the Soviet Union than in some states in America. Although the average Soviet citizen does not believe in God and although the Communists do not hesitate to use any means to further world revolution, one cannot say that the Russians are immoral in their daily relations with each other (except on the political and official level, where diplomatic lies are common).

As a people, the Russians are humane. They love children and have special department stores for them. They have special restaurants for women with children; they have special seats in streetcars and buses for women with children and for invalids. They like to be in crowds and enjoy close physical contact. Girls embrace each other frequently and are quick to shed tears; even men kiss each other or hold hands in comradely fashion.

The foreign visitor, who at the beginning of the 1960's stood sharply apart by his dress, now more and more blends into the Soviet scene in a large city. Soviet tourists, who are beginning to travel abroad, likewise do not attract attention by their appearance. In the years following the Communist Revolution it was regarded as fashionable to look like a worker, and women expressed their equality by shunning make-up and feminine hairdos and by wearing masculine suits and drab dresses. Now girls wearing make-up and styled hairdos, in blue, maroon, or black stockings and high heels and trim nylon raincoats, stroll arm in arm with young men in drip-dry shirts and narrow-trousered suits. As they go to the theaters and cafés, eat caviar and drink champagne, dance the latest steps, and walk down the streets with their transistor radios blaring, they look more and more like young people in the United States.

TWELVE

EPILOGUE

It is important for Americans to expose the shortcomings of communism, but merely to expose them is not enough. Many who support the Communist cause are aware of the hardships and oppression of Communist rule. Yet they remain supporters, for they believe that stern measures are necessary to combat the injustices and shortcomings of their own society. To outlaw communism will not suffice. It will bolster the Communist argument that Communists are fighting for freedom and will dramatize the role of Communists as heroes willing to suffer for their ideals.

To halt the spread of communism it is necessary to understand the reasons for its existence and to do away with the conditions on which it thrives. Remove poverty, economic insecurity, and social and racial discrimination and you will have deprived communism of much of its appeal. Generally speaking, communism attracts mass support where the people have "nothing to lose but their chains." It is essential, furthermore, to feed the mind with purpose, be it the building of a better society or simply the leading of a good life. Communist leadership is provided by intellectuals, often from well-to-do families. Whether these men are genuinely motivated by Communist ideology or use it as a means to personal power, they join ideals with bread as weapons in the struggle for men's loyalties. "Where there is plenty of bread and a shortage of ideals, bread is no substitute for an ideal," Yevgeny Yevtushenko notes. "But where bread is short, ideals are bread." [23]

The Communist threat to the free world has its military aspects, as the Korean War, the Cuban missile crisis, and the Vietnam conflict have shown. The West cannot afford to lower its military guard and must be ever ready to meet force with force. But bullets alone or bullets and bread alone cannot kill ideas. The superiority of the democratic way of life must be demonstrated by success at home. If democracy will provide greater political freedom and economic security and will prove effective in coping with crime, juvenile delinquency, and international conflict, the people of the world will be attracted to it rather than to communism.

Recent years have brought significant changes in the Soviet Union. Stalin has been removed from the mausoleum, and Khrushchev, who began the process of de-Stalinization, has himself been deposed, though—and this, too, is a sign of change—he has not been executed and is allowed to live a relatively normal life in retirement.

At the moment no one person dominates the Soviet scene. Generally, pictures of Brezhnev and Kosygin and one or more people are displayed, though occasionally one or the other appears singly. For example, a student dormitory whose front wall was decorated for the first of May, 1961, with Khrushchev showed Brezhnev on the same occasion in 1965.

Inside the university dormitories, too, there have been changes. Rooms that in 1961 were decorated primarily with pictures of Khrushchev, Castro, and Gagarin now have pictures of movie stars and jazz musicians. One student in 1965 adorned his walls with large photographs of Robert Kennedy, John F. Kennedy, Winston Churchill, and Ray Charles. There is freer discussion by students of the meaning of communism, socialism, and other political philosophies. Yet at the same time there is less concern with politics and greater concern with life and creativity. Writers, poets, and artists express themselves more freely.

This is not to say that Russian society is at last free. The controls of power are essentially the same. But this makes the exploration of the young people the more admirable. If the process of loosening up continues, it will be due to their courage, as well as to the decision of the men at the helm of the state. Older intellectuals, too, are more willing to associate with foreign scholars and to invite them into their homes. Where contact with foreigners was once feared, it is now more acceptable. In general, the foreigner has become less of a spectacle and menace. The government welcomes him increasingly as a tourist to obtain needed foreign currency.

In economic affairs, also, there is some experimentation. The reexamination of Communist theories and actions is pragmatic—experiences rather than doctrines are cited. A lag in Soviet production has led to the adoption of a number of capitalist incentives.

The matter-of-factness with which the first of

The first of May is a time for fun as well as dedication. Colorful balloons are popular with young and old.

May is celebrated by the people is surprising to the American visitor. To be sure, everybody congratulates everybody with the holiday. Offices and stores are closed for two days, gifts are exchanged, much alcohol is consumed, and the cities are decorated with placards and flags. Yet the political spirit and enthusiasm seem faded. As the demonstrators walked past the reviewing stands in Leningrad on May 1, 1965, the loudspeakers behind the stands blared forth a continuous series of hails for Soviet women, the Soviet military, and "our native Soviet government" together with background cheers over the same loudspeaker. The people who walked past responded here and there with some cheers, but without much enthusiasm. After more than forty years the slogans had become tired and stale.

The gigantic victory celebration on May 9, 1965, in honor of the twentieth anniversary of the defeat of Germany emphasized the increasingly patriotic trend of communism. In Eastern Europe and in China, too, nationalistic feeling had taken hold of the Communist movement and had led to disputes among Communist states.

While the split in the Communist camp may not be more severe than the split in the Western alliance, its effect may be beneficial for all concerned. When the United States and the Soviet Union dominated the international scene without challenge from other powers in the years after World War II, every controversy was complicated by the problem of preserving prestige and "face." Neither was able to back down gracefully. As disputes cease to be confined to a confrontation between East and West and as debates and compromises become common within each camp, chances may be improved for recognizing and accepting different views and approaches. The possibility may be increased—as President Kennedy hoped—to make the world "safe for diversity."

NOTES

[1] Wright W. Miller, *Russians as People* (New York: E. P. Dutton & Co., Inc., 1961), p. 18.

[2] *Ibid.*, pp. 29-30.

[3] Louis Fischer, *The Life of Lenin* (New York: Harper & Row, Publishers, 1964), p. 43.

[4] Nicholas V. Riasanovsky, *A History of Russia* (New York: Oxford University Press, 1963), p. 520.

[5] Edward Crankshaw, in the *St. Petersburg Times,* October 4, 1965, p. 16A.

[6] A. Denisov and M. Kirichenko, *Soviet State Law* (Moscow: Foreign Language Publishing House, 1960), p. 405.

[7] Vissarion Belinsky, *Selected Philosophical Works* (Moscow: Foreign Languages Publishing House, 1956), pp. 537-538.

[8] *Life,* Vol. 55, No. 11 (September 13, 1963), Special Issue about the Soviet people, p. 37.

[9] Anatole G. Mazour, *Russia Tsarist and Communist* (Princeton, N.J.: D. Van Nostrand Company, Inc., 1962), pp. 469-470.

[10] Marc Slonim, *The Epic of Russian Literature from Its Origins Through Tolstoi* (New York: Oxford University Press, 1950), p. 82.

[11] Thomas Riha, ed., *Readings in Russian Civilization* (Chicago: The University of Chicago Press, 1964), pp. 313-314.

[12] Slonim, p. 112.

[13] Leo Tolstoy, *Count Tolstoy on the War Between Russia and Japan. "Bethink Yourselves"* (New York: Frederick A. Stokes, n.d.), pp. 53-54 and 57-58.

[14] Hans Kohn, *The Mind of Modern Russia: Historical and Political Thought of Russia's Great Age* (New York: Harper & Row, Publishers, 1955), p. 157.

[15] Abram Tertz, *On Socialist Realism* (New York: Random House, Inc., 1960), pp. 36-37.

[16] Valerij Bryusov, "Mowers in the Line of Fire," from *Russian Poetry 1917-1955,* trans. by Jack Lindsay (London: The Bodley Head Ltd., 1957), pp. 23-24.

[17] Tertz, p. 66.

[18] Henri Troyat, *Pushkin: His Life and Times,* trans. by Randolph T. Weaver (New York: Random House, Inc., 1950), p. 415. Poem translated by Babette Deutsch.

[19] Vera Aleksandrova, *A History of Soviet Literature 1917-1962* (Garden City, N.Y.: Doubleday & Company, Inc., 1963), p. 332.

[20] Boris Pasternak, "The Nobel Prize," from *Poems* by Boris Pasternak, trans. by Eugene M. Kayden (Yellow Springs, Ohio: The Antioch Press, 1964), p. 300.

[21] Semyon Kirsanov, "Simplicity," from *Russian Poetry 1917-1955,* trans. by Jack Lindsay (London: The Bodley Head Ltd., 1957), pp. 136-137.

[22] Arthur E. Adams, ed., *Readings in Soviet Foreign Policy: Theory and Practice* (Boston: D. C. Heath and Company, 1961), p. 43.

[23] Yevgenii Yevtushenko, "A Precocious Autobiography," trans. by Andrew R. MacAndrew, *The Saturday Evening Post,* Vol. 236, No. 38 (August 10-17, 1963), p. 54.

FOR ADDITIONAL READING

Books available in paperback are preceded by an asterisk (*); the paperback publisher is listed in parentheses.

* Adams, Arthur E., ed., *Readings in Soviet Foreign Policy: Theory and Practice.* Boston: D. C. Heath and Company, 1961. A collection of articles and documents.

* Alexandrova, Vera, *A History of Soviet Literature 1917-1962.* Garden City, N.Y.: Doubleday & Company, Inc., 1963 (Anchor). A detailed account of the trends in Russian literature since the Revolution.

Browder, Robert Paul, and Kerensky, Alexander F., eds., *The Russian Provisional Government 1917.* Stanford: Stanford University Press, 1961, 3 vols. The first volume of this large collection of documents contains a readable account of the February Revolution of 1917.

* Cambell, Robert W., *Soviet Economic Power.* Boston: Houghton Mifflin Company, 1960. A nontechnical account of how the Soviet economy functions.

Crankshaw, Edward, *Russia and the Russians.* New York: The Viking Press, Inc., 1948. A readable description and interpretation of the Soviet Union at the beginning of the cold war.

* ———, *The New Cold War: Moscow v. Peking.*

Baltimore: Penguin Books, Inc., 1963. A brief survey of the Sino–Soviet dispute.

* Cressey, George B., *Soviet Potentials: A Geographic Appraisal.* Syracuse, N.Y.: Syracuse University Press, 1962. A readable introduction to the regions and resources of the Soviet Union.

Dallin, Alexander, comp., *Soviet Conduct in World Affairs.* New York: Columbia University Press, 1960. A collection of readings on Soviet foreign policy and its formulation.

Deane, John R., *The Strange Alliance.* New York: The Viking Press, Inc., 1947. A readable account of the negotiations and experiences of an American general in the Soviet Union during World War II.

* Florinsky, Michael T., *The End of the Russian Empire.* New York: Collier Books, 1961. An account of the events from the 1890's to 1917 leading to the downfall of the Russian monarchy.

* Fullard, Harold, ed., *Soviet Union in Maps.* Chicago: Denoyer-Geppert, 1961. An inexpensive collection of maps in color, depicting the history, topography, climate, and economy of Russia and the Soviet Union.

Gray, Camilla, *The Great Experiment: Russian Art 1863-1922.* New York: Harry N. Abrams, Inc., 1962. An illustrated study of modern art in Russia.

Hamilton, George Heard, *The Art and Architecture of Russia.* Baltimore: Penguin Books, Inc., 1954. A detailed historical survey to the end of the nineteenth century.

Harcave, Sidney, *Russia: A History,* 5th ed. Philadelphia: J. B. Lippincott Company, 1964. A standard textbook.

* Harkins, William E., *Dictionary of Russian Literature*. New York: Philosophical Library, Inc., 1956 (Littlefield, Adams, and Co.). A useful reference work.

* Hazard, John N., *The Soviet System of Government*, rev. ed. Chicago: The University of Chicago Press, 1960. A readable account of the structure and workings of the Soviet government.

* Hechinger, Fred M., *The Big Red Schoolhouse*. Garden City, N.Y.: Doubleday & Company, Inc., 1959. Comparison between Russian and American educational policies and developments.

* Hunt, Robert N. C., *The Theory and Practice of Communism: An Introduction*. New York: The Macmillan Company, 1957. An examination of Communist doctrine from Marx and Engels through Stalin.

Karpovich, Michael, *Imperial Russia, 1801-1917*. New York: Holt, Rinehart and Winston, Inc., 1932. A brief survey of imperial Russian history, criticizing failures and praising achievements.

* Kohn, Hans, ed., *The Mind of Modern Russia: Historical and Political Thought of Russia's Great Age*. New York: Harper & Row, Publishers, 1955 (Harper Torchbooks). A very convenient little collection of readings.

* Lerche, Charles O., Jr., *The Cold War and After*. Englewood Cliffs, N.J.: Prentice-Hall, Inc., 1965. A thought-provoking analysis of shifting patterns in American–Soviet relations.

Lindsay, Jack, trans., *Russian Poetry 1917-1955*. London: The Bodley Head, 1957. A convenient collection.

* McNeal, Robert H., *The Bolshevik Tradition: Lenin,*

Stalin, Khrushchev. Englewood Cliffs, N.J.: Prentice-Hall, Inc., 1963. Depicts the leaders and issues in the three major stages of development of the Communist party in the Soviet Union.

* ———, ed., *Lenin, Stalin, Khrushchev: Voices of Bolshevism.* Englewood Cliffs, N.J.: Prentice-Hall, Inc., 1963. A collection of writings and speeches, supplementing and illustrating *The Bolshevik Tradition.*

* Mamatey, Victor S., *Soviet Russian Imperialism.* New York: D. Van Nostrand Company, Inc., 1964 (Anvil). A collection of documents with an historical introduction.

* Mehlinger, Howard D., ed., *Communism in Theory and Practice.* San Francisco: Chandler Publishing Company, 1964. A book of readings for high school students.

* Mehnert, Klaus, *Soviet Man and His World,* trans. from the German by Maurice Rosenbaum. New York: Frederick A. Praeger, Inc., 1962. A readable account of Soviet attitudes and ways.

Miller, Wright, *Russians as People.* New York: E. P. Dutton & Co., Inc., 1961. A beautifully written portrayal of daily life in the Soviet Union.

* Mosse, W. E., *Alexander II and the Modernization of Russia.* New York: Collier Books, 1962. A readable account of the life and times of the "Tsar Liberator."

Rice, Tamara Talbot, *A Concise History of Russian Art.* New York: Frederick A. Praeger, Inc., 1963. A beautifully illustrated popular survey going up to the Revolution.

* Rieber, Alfred J., and Nelson, Robert C., *A Study of the U.S.S.R. and Communism: An Historical Ap-*

proach. Chicago: Scott, Foresman and Company, 1962. A brief survey for high school use.

* ———, eds., *The U.S.S.R. and Communism: Source Readings and Interpretations.* Chicago: Scott, Foresman and Company, 1964. Brief selections for high school students.

* Rosen, Seymour M., *Higher Education in the U.S.S.R. Curriculum, Schools, and Statistics.* Washington: U.S. Government Printing Office, 1963. A straightforward survey with many statistical tables.

Rubinstein, Alvin Z., ed., *The Foreign Policy of the Soviet Union.* New York: Random House, Inc., 1960. A collection of documents.

Schwartz, Harry, *The Soviet Economy Since Stalin.* Philadelphia: J. B. Lippincott Company, 1965. A vivid account of Soviet economic development from 1953 to 1964.

* Scott, Derek J. R., *Russian Political Institutions.* New York: Frederick A. Praeger, Inc., 1961. An examination of Russian politics and administration.

* Seton-Watson, Hugh, *From Lenin to Khrushchev: The History of World Communism.* New York: Frederick A. Praeger, Inc., 1960. A readable historical survey of events in the Soviet Union and in Eastern Europe.

* Shub, David, *Lenin: A Biography,* abridged by Donald Porter Geddes. New York: New American Library of World Literature, Inc., 1951 (Mentor). A readable, brief account of the founder of the Soviet Union.

* Slonim, Marc, *An Outline of Russian Literature.* New York: Oxford University Press, 1958 (Men-

tor). A brief survey of Russian literature from its origins to the Revolution of 1917.

* Taaffe, Robert N., and Kingsbury, Robert C., *An Atlas of Soviet Affairs*. New York: Frederick A. Praeger, Inc., 1965. A most useful collection of simple maps and text on various aspects of the Soviet Union.

Treadgold, Donald W., *Lenin and His Rivals: The Struggle for Russia's Future, 1898-1906*. New York: Frederick A. Praeger, Inc., 1955. A study of rival political views in the years before and during the Revolution of 1905.

* Turgenev, Ivan S., *A Sportsman's Notebook*, trans. by Charles and Natasha Hepburn. New York: The Viking Press, Inc., 1957 (Compass). Sketches of nineteenth-century peasant and country life shortly before the emancipation of the serfs.

* Utechin, S. V., ed., *Everyman's Concise Encyclopedia of Russia*. New York: E. P. Dutton & Co., Inc., 1961. A handy reference work, though uneven in coverage.

* Wallace, Sir Donald Mackenzie, *Russia on the Eve of War and Revolution*. New York: Vintage Books, Inc., 1961. A contemporary description of life and conditions in prerevolutionary Russia.

* Whiting, Kenneth R., *The Soviet Union Today: A Concise Handbook*. New York: Frederick A. Praeger, Inc., 1962. Chapters on such topics as people, government, leadership, agriculture, industry, and armed forces.

Yarmolinsky, Avrahm, ed., *The Poems, Prose and Plays of Alexander Pushkin*. New York: The Modern Library, Inc., 1936. An anthology of the writings of Russia's greatest poet.

* Yevtushenko, Yevgenii, *A Precocious Autobiography*, trans. by Andrew R. MacAndrew. New York: E. P. Dutton & Co., Inc., 1964. The recollections and thoughts of a young and outspoken Soviet poet.

———, *Yevtushenko: Selected Poems*. New York: E. P. Dutton & Co., Inc., 1962 (Penguin Books). A collection of poems about Soviet life.

A more detailed annotated list of books on the Soviet Union will be found in *Russia and the Soviet Union: A Bibliographic Guide to Western-Language Publications* (Chicago: The University of Chicago Press, 1965), edited by Paul L. Horecky. To keep abreast of new publications, the reader should consult the *Slavic Review*, a quarterly of Soviet and East European Studies, and the *Russian Review*, a quarterly devoted to Russian culture, which contain book reviews not generally found in newspapers and popular magazines. The annual *American Bibliography of Russian and East European Studies*, published like the *Slavic Review* by the American Association for the Advancement of Slavic Studies, gives a listing of articles and books arranged by topic. *The Current Digest of the Soviet Press* provides a running survey of the Soviet point of view.

INDEX